Morning Storm Devotional

A Devotional Guide and Declaration for Acceleration in Your Life

By: Apostle Dr. Nichole Masters

Morning Storm Devotional

ISBN: 978-1-990266-64-5

Printed in the USA by:

by God's Grace i Stand

My Walk of Faith

Dedication

Morning Storm is dedicated to those who are hungry and thirsty for more of the super-natural power and glory of God, and are ready for accelerated growth and development in every department of their life. According to the Oxford dictionary, a storm is *a violent disturbance of the atmosphere with strong winds and usually rain, thunder, lightning, or snow. A tumultuous reaction and uproar.* On the day of Pentecost (Acts 2:2) the Holy Spirit was poured out on the disciples like a "*rushing mighty wind.*" They encountered fire, power and glory like never before. Morning Storm will disturb, challenge, shift and accelerate you from ordinary to extra-ordinary as you stand in your God given authority.

Many faithful Christians who love God, live under untold hardships and sufferings because they are ignorant of who they are. The Word of God declares in St. Luke 10:19 KJV, "Behold I give unto you power to tread on serpents and scorpions, and over all the power of the enemy; and nothing shall by any means hurt you." Jesus empowered his disciples to become aware of their authority that the Father has given them back in Genesis, to be fruitful, multiply, replenish, subdue and take dominion in the earth. The enemy comes to kill, steal and destroy, and that is the reason many believers are suffering such great loss. But when you are aware of your authority and dominion and that you were made in the image and likeness of God, you enforce His laws by opening your mouth and declaring the word of life with power and authority over your circumstances. You will experience a shift and acceleration in your life, and demons must bow and let go off your stuff.

Acknowledgements

I am eternally grateful to my God my Lord and Saviour Jesus Christ who has divinely inspired me through the power of the Holy Spirit to pen this devotional. He gave me enduring strength that I could only find in Him.

This devotional was birthed in one of the most turbulent and stormy periods of my life in ministry. Dealing with a heart-rending betrayal in the worst possible way, from a prominent leader in the ministry; facing persecutions from high authorities who were determined that the church cannot stay at its present location in Stony Hill, St. Andrew, Jamaica, it was warfare on every side. The traumatic journey of my new-born grand-baby Emma, who was born pre-matured weighing a little over two pounds. She had to be resuscitated seven times. The evil reports said her leg had to be amputated, her veins were bursting and at one point the doctors could not locate a ventilator suitable for her tiny body. But this pushed me into the labour room of prayer, the Holy Spirit told me one was located. Shortly after prayer my daughter-in-law reported a ventilator was found, the doctors concluded that this must be a miracle child. She was named the miracle baby by the doctors.

But thanks to the overwhelming support of my family, namely: my husband, Minister Robert Masters Snr. and children Nicoy, Tyreek and Robert Jnr, mother Joyce Witter, sister and armor bearer Shellion Livingstone, Kerry-Ann Masters and my miracle grand-daughter baby Emma. These wonderful individuals pushed me through the process.

Special thanks to: Minister Josephine Barton, Evangelist Janet Clarke-Christian, Bishop Tamie-Zoe McPherson, Reverend David Schleifer, Sister Beverly Walters, and my church family, Miracles of the Potter's Hand International for their invaluable support.

Thanks to Bishop McPherson and all the other persons who provided moral and spiritual support for the journey.

Introduction

In the very early years of my journey with the Lord, I had a searing passion to know him and so I began to seek Him earnestly. I would spend hours and hours in prayer before the Lord, and as a result I had multiple super-natural encounters with God. These encounters opened up an insatiable appetite in me for the Word of God and its practical application in my life. Because of these encounters I refused to be an ordinary Christian, I wanted more. There were too many people suffering around me and I was not impressed with that life because it did not represent my God. My bowels of compassion were stirred up to see people loosed, healed, delivered and set free from every boundedness in their lives. I wanted to see them walk in the original plan God had intended for them.

The title of this book manifested when someone who read my first devotional, Morning Dew was greatly impacted by it to the point where they exclaimed, "this is Morning Storm!"

This devotional is designed to empower you and open the eyes of your understanding to your authority as a dual citizen of heaven and earth. This is where you stand in the earth realm and command things in the heavens to respond to you and they must comply because you have applied the laws of the kingdom.

Table of Contents

Part 1
Devotionals

"Be not conformed to this world but be ye transformed by the renewing of the mind."

Romans 12:2

What area or areas of your life do you need to experience newness? Perhaps you have not felt any real change in any area of your life; or maybe you have become a connoisseur/(expert) of change, experiencing success after success, but one area just seems to elude you; similar to the most decorated Olympian who has never won a gold medal. What you need at this point is a SHIFT. Many persons feel stuck in an area of their life and believe they are helpless. You have tried many things including fasting and prayer but your life remains the same. As you lift your faith, Morning Storm will catapult you from where you are to where you need to be.

Day One

The Just Man Shall Live by Faith I

Scripture: Hebrews 11:1 – 6

The just shall live by faith. However, some of us do not have faith. Many of us are in church but we do not exercise our God given faith, according to Romans 12:3,"…God has given to every man a measure of faith." The bible declares that, "Without faith it is impossible to please God" (Hebrews 11:6 KJV). If you are going to serve God your faith must be lifted to a super-natural level, to believe a supreme being and counsellor that you have never seen. You have never seen this God but you serve him. You may ask, "How do I serve a God whom I have never seen? How do I grow spiritually into the fullness of this God that I have never seen? How do I spend hours trying to pursue an invisible God?" My! My!

You need to understand that the more you seek is the more you will find. In the first place, acknowledging God requires that you must believe that He is (God). If you do not believe you cannot worship a God that you have never seen; neither can you follow his laws and precepts. And so John's gospel was about the miracles, signs and the wonders that God did for man to believe. The bible said,

"The disciples were in a ship and there was a wind that became so boisterous that they began to cry out, Lord! Lord!" Because they were ignorant of the fact that they could rebuke the wind they called on Jesus and Jesus responded, "O you of little faith." You have been with me so long, but where is your faith?

Faith looks irrational and may seem like foolishness. You can have a current situation and the devil knows that, and he messes with your meds/mediation just for you to make the wrong decision. But if you can grab faith and hold on to it, you will matriculate into someone great. That is why there is no greatness in a lot of us because we lack faith. The hour has come for man to step over into greatness. I feel with every fiber of my being that God is about to call for a great revival and some miracles and it takes faith.

I am laughing in my spirit because of the things that God is saying. If God is saying it, it means that somebody reading the *Morning Storm Devotional* has this same posture of faith to grab it and run with it.

I don't care what you are going through, what the doctor said about you but if you can grab it and run with it. Some miraculous testimonies are coming. Somebody say revelation! One revelation can change an entire nation, and the entire course of your life. Do you think I am joking? Some of you may be doing domestic work/household helper earning Ten thousand ($10,000) or Fifteen thousand ($15,000) Jamaican dollars per week. However, if God gives you one revelation how to create wealth you would never do another domestic job. Some of you are taking the medication but if God gives you a revelation, you will not have to purchase another pill.

We are in the time and season where God wants to talk to His people and alot of people have sold out themselves to some strange things in this life because they cannot wait on God. I recalled when I just got saved, I prayed about who I wanted to be in God and I said "Lord I do not want to be an ordinary person or Christian. I want to be something great." The devil heard and he showed me an old ratoon (*Jamaican term for someone who shows no progress or growth in a particular area of life, despite having years of exposure*) who was saved from childhood.

"He said, look at this person there is no greatness in him, and nothing has become of him, Do you think you just got saved and you are going to become someone great? I said, "Lord I don't care, I want to become someone great." I lived to see this same person (ratoon) applauding me saying, "You are a mighty woman of God and I desire to have the grace that is upon your life."

First John 4:4 KJV declares, "*Ye are of God, little children, and have overcome them: because greater is he that is in you, than he that is in the world.*" Therefore you can be what you want to be in God because of the Greater that is in you. Shout! Greater is in my belly!

The just man shall live by his faith. What is faith? The word of God declares, in Hebrews 11:1 KJV, *Faith is the substance of things hoped for but the evidence of things not seen.* I don't see it but I believe that God can do it. I would like to ask a question because there are all kinds of people (in church). If you are a person who is unable to read, and because of this limiting, earthly situation, you have no use for God, that is a lie! Some people believe because they cannot exegete, eisegete or is the greatest theologian, they behave as if they are written off. The enemy has some people in derision/bound because they don't think they have the ability to help God but God does not need your help. God wants to help you.

You think you do not have the ability to do what an apostle can do but he/she was just available. God only needs your availability, your love and your pure attention. God needs you to be you and he will use you for his glory.

God spoke to Moses who grew up in Egypt and was a part of the Egyptian system for many years; But He called out Moses for a task. God called out many of us for a task; but we choose to do what we want to do because we think that we are not capable. But the time and the hour we begin to see God as God then our mindset will change. We need a face to face encounter with God and when we get that encounter our lives can never be the same again. A man who is unable to read, his condition does not stop him from loving God, seeking God, having faith in God. We declare that if you are such a one you shall have double for your trouble. Now every 'crosses' that the enemy put on your life from a child, we rebuke it by fire! May God deliver you from the strong hold of the enemy and give you victory.

A person's inability to read may limit him from doing certain earthly things, but spiritually there are no boundaries. When a man loves God and is not intelligent the Holy Ghost can teach him to read; as it was the Holy Spirit who taught me to drive. I was a 'scary cat.' But when I went around the steering wheel and I spoke to God that hour. I prayed, "God you have to let me drive for you because I want to go on mission. I am tired of waiting on my husband to drive me around.

Today I drive confidently and go anywhere I want to go. Sometimes my children say, “Mommy your foot is heavy,” because of how hard I press gas without fear. Before I became a driver my husband told me he did not need a conductor because when he drove too hard I would beat the side of the vehicle with my hand. Recently I was travelling and a truck was on my side, so I swerved the vehicle from the truck and the truck was still coming towards me. And I had to swerve out of it another time. I am no longer scared because the spirit of the Lord is upon me and *I can do all things through Christ who strengthens me,* (Phillipians 4:13 KJV).

Confession

Holy Father, I humbly approach your throne. Declaring that you are the Most Holy God and there is none like you, neither in this life nor the one to come. My Father, I am grateful for your written word abounding with examples of great men and women of Faith, especially Hebrews 11. Lord when I examine my life in the mirror of your word I confess that oftentimes I doubt when I have no reason to. I ask you oh Father, to burn and destroy every seed and root of doubt and fear in me. Wash me in your blood and set me free, in Jesus mighty name.

Day Two

The Just Man Shall Live by Faith II

Scripture: Exodus 14:20 – 31

The bible declares that big and strong pharaoh had authority over Israel for many years, but God had a plan. I would like to address a sheep; know that God has a plan for you. God is with you. The devil makes it appears as though nothing is going on for you; but some of us need to get in our position of authority and say, "Listen now devil, *mi a chat back to you*. You used to slap me but now I am slapping you back. Come with your slime, big eyes, scary behavior, host of hell, I don't care how many demons accompany you." My God says, "*Whatever I bind on earth is bound in heaven and whatsoever, I loose on earth is loosed in heaven,*" (St. Matthew 18:18 KJV). Lord go before me as fire by night and cloud by day. Who can stop you? Fire! Arise with your faith because you are not ordinary, and ensure that you cause problems in the earth. Make certain that you destroy up some balm yards, break up some strange altars, and destroy some generational curses. Some evil cycles, exes, vexes, jinxes, spells. Do not die ordinary.

If you desire to drive and you do not have a license go and obtain it. If you do not have the money to buy the vehicle, purchase a tyre and put it under your bed, or where you can see it. Declare, "I must own a car because I serve Jesus the risen King." Some of you will go in some car marts without a dollar and say "grace and favour is running after me. In the name of Jesus I like this one." Do not look at the cost before you like it. Like what you like and then you purchase what you like. If you are serving God then you are not limited, Zion arise!

There are some young women and men, when they are choosing lovers they want rich people. They pick and choose by the process of elimination until they have found the right person. When they have found the love of their life, they say this one can work and they step into the relationship. They are moving by their faith, so what says you who carry the mark of Jesus Christ upon you? Your father owns cattle upon a thousand hills, Psalm 50:10 KJV. If you are really serving God, do you believe you can speak to God about something? Declaring God this is what I desire and it happens? If you do not believe it then you are not ready for this level of faith. Stop aiming low, go higher. The more the anointing takes you higher, is the higher you must soar like the eagle. The eagle is not intimidated by the wind it allows the wind to push it higher and so the greater the wind blows is the higher the eagle soars.

You believe God can heal from a flu symptom but what about cancer? Diabetes? Some of you need to go on a hospital visit. You are not going to a specific patient but somebody is in there. When you walk in there something has to happen. You need to pray and something happens. Prayer warrior you spend over an hour on the phone in your casual conversations with friends but you are on the altar only ten minutes with God, that cannot work. Let go of the things of the world and cleave to the Jesus Christ the Rock. We have some things to cross over into. There are Some red seas that need to be dried up and situations that need to be rebuked.

The bible declared that Pharoah met Moses but Moses had nothing in his hand except his rod. What do you have in your hands today that you can use? Some of you may be confused reading this as you have never thought this way before. The hour has come for a greater revival. You can't stay in one position all the days of your life. You have to rise up, enough is enough. Some of you are saved ten years and you can't pray for someone and they get healing. That is not God. It is your life that is not right.

God gave us the power and authority, St. Luke 10:18. Some of you are saved five years and you cannot pray a simple opening prayer in public? We are missing the best part of what God has in store and those who are looking in do not want to be a part of what we are displaying, it is not appealing. When a man becomes a Satanist he has to drink the blood. He wakes up at 12 mid-night and for the rest of the night he is a zombie. If he is required to eat flesh he will eat it. I read about a man in Africa who was a Satanist and he had to have sex on the grave as a part of the ritual. These are not an easy set of people. When a man hates God he hates God. He is filled with legions, demonic forces. Sometimes when persons come before a deliverance minister, what they are coming with is not normal. They walk with hell. Do you know how? They intentionally engage in their evil practices and they make sacrifices.

Do not believe that a man who is a Satanist, lodge man, and all those deviant behaviours just signed a piece of paper and that is it.

They have to do the rituals to bring on the evil upon them. Those of you who love Zionist, obeah man, sorcerers and love to go and seek, it is Satan who is speaking through these people. They spent quality time sacrificing to have all kinds of powers upon them. The higher they go the more in depths their rituals become. It is the reason some of them reach the place where they have to now kill people. When you are in God and converted, you think you can simply baptize and say that is it? You have to fast and pray and give up some things. The more you fast and pray is the more you get empowered. The more you are honest to God, understand the word is the more you experience growth.

A Christian must be different, if you are arrogant you need deliverance. It is dumbfounding what some Christians do in church. God will not use persons who are full of nasty attitude. The flesh has to die first. When you start to read and understand the word, fast, pray you will know how to live better. The word is going to guide you. The more you become a type of Christ is the more the glory is upon you.

Moses had a task. The bible tells us that Pharaoh was now advancing at Israel. Moses cried out to God. There were mountains on the left and right, Pharaoh and his armies behind them and before them was a big sea. God asked Moses, "What do you have in your hand?"

It takes God for you to get a breakthrough when you are in that situation. It is either you compromise, go back where you are coming from or you lift your faith and allow the power of God to manifest. Ask yourself, What do I have in my hand? Some of you are so distracted by other people's giftings that you become confused. You are so fixated on what somebody else is doing but you can't focus on what God wants to do in you. Some of you become guilty of identity theft. You are stealing other people's personality. But what is it that you have that can bring glory to God?

You may become bound by a limitation you have, eg. Inability to read. It is not what you are able to do well but what God can do through you. There are a lot of persons who were incarcerated and were unable to read but God helped them over that hurdle. Many have testified of their victory over that handicap. They learnt to read in prison. What is it that cause you to be so limited that you cannot do anything for God? This question is to provoke you in the spirit. Why can't you be available for God to use you? A lot of you have too many excuses. All God needs is your full attention. Are you sleeping at this point?

What Moses had in his hand was a piece of stick, a rod. Some of you can pray even though you cannot find words. But you realize that you can stay on your knees for a long while although you keep repeating the same things, it means you are an intercessor. Some of you have a passion to pray, you can stay on your belly for hours, pay some attention to that. If you can't sing, do not crow, leave the singers' business alone. If you are a preacher, take the microphone from the singers and preach! Stay in your lane. Do not watch apostle who can jump in the anointing, outside of that they she is very heavy. If you try that and it was not given to you, you may break a leg. But God can send you to teach and you flow. What is it that you have in your hand? Do not say that you can't. what can you do for God? You are not going to sit down every day. What can you do for the king your master?

Confession

Oh my exalted Father, I approach your throne naked and ashamed. I ask for your forgiveness of all the times when I became fearful and doubted you in the moment. You are not a man to lie nor the son of man to repent. Therefore I offended you by my action. I repent for satisfying my flesh and not obeying your word. I receive your forgiveness in Jesus Mighty name, Amen.

Day Three

Practical Faith Walk

Scripture: Exodus 14:20 – 27; Exodus 33:6 – 10

God is here to give His people solution but they are often distracted by what they don't have. Trouble came to Israel, they were blocked on every side, before and behind. Many times this is how the enemy puts you in a position to sin against God. Where is your faith? Maybe God is saying put on the pot on the fire and wait on the food to come. In the interim sing, Rock of Ages cleft for me The Lord asked Moses, What do you have in your hand? Some of you have some uncommon worship and entertain angels when you open your mouth. You have something in your throat that is connected to angels. What do you want? Say more of you God. This key is revelation to your faith walk.

What do you have in your hand that you can use to get you out of your dire situation? Stop waiting on bigger and mightier. You may say that you have no food in your house but you can find a little flour, a tiny bit of oil, two different pieces of meat. Cook a little soup, or cook some slide and whine (*dumpling made from flour and butter – indigenous to Jamaica*). Stop complaining and use what you have in your hand. Do not hide your rod and borrow your neighbour's rod. Whatever God gave you, that is what you must use. God says *I will not leave you comfortless*...St. John 14:18 KJV. Use what you have in your hand, if you have a scripture use it and shoot down the devil. He wants you to be paranoid, go down in deep depression.

The enemy pursued after the Israelites. I submit to you today that the smallest thing that you have in your hand you can use it. That is what will bring down the enemy. You can be on your knees for an hour and all you are doing is pleading the blood! The blood! The blood of Jesus in my house, in the baby crib, it is your most potent weapon. Maybe you are so emotional that you go before Jesus and keep bawling Jesus, Jesus, Jesus. The power of God will hoist you up.

Moses went through a lot but his attitude is admirable. Some of you would have murmured and complained, God you sent me on your assignment but you are *styling me* (to disrespect or under-rate). How do you think you can be used up in the body of Christ or on the street? it is by faith. Simply copying what somebody else does hides your true identity and robs God of his glory. What is it that you always have a passion for? What is it that you feel when something happens and you know this is God's calling for your life? As you think about it and it comes to mind, that is your solution, that is what God is going to use.

Moses saw God and came face to face with him. No man can see God and live so do not think about a physical encounter as we know it. But he came in contact with God in his splendor and glory. When Moses stretched out what he had in his hand, the red sea immediately parted and all of Israel crossed over on dry land. When they were safely on the other side, Pharaoh and all the enemies that rose up against Israel pursued them with determination. God commanded Moses to stretch out what he had in his hand. This time the red sea receded to its original state and covered all of Pharaoh and his men and killed them. Today God is saying, "There is something in you." Let this sink deep in your spirit. There is something in you that can bring glory to his name and bring deliverance to a nation. At this point I am feeling challenged in the realms of the spirit for some people whose faith is not yet at the level. I am still feeling your sense of dependency. Come on, come on. Arise and lift your faith. This is the hour of your solution.

If God is doing great and mighty things then revival must break out in the church, the faith of God's people must be risen. One of the things Moses did in chapter 33:6 – 9 of Exodus, was worshipped and the people saw. They began to position themselves as well to worship God. They noticed something, when Moses went in the tabernacle the pillar of cloud would come and stand. This is glory! I am here to declare war on your behalf. Pharoah the enemy, has held you captive for too long. God wants to deliver you out of the hands of Phaoraoh's bondage. Some of you are coming from some poverty-stricken bloodline. Nobody can help anybody.

God has some Joseph to bring deliverance to the blood line. If you do not position yourself to use what is in your hand, How are you going to deliver your people? There are some blood-line where no one has ever been to college but it is your children who are going to college. Do you know why? Because you are a warrior, you are fighting for them. Your eyes were blinded like theirs but now you realize it is not business as usual. You realize that no one is birthing out because of the stronghold that has them but God is going to use you to break them free. God has given some people responsibility, authority. Some of us have some relationship with God when we go down to pray, something has to break. This is your cue. Yes you, I am speaking to you.

Yes! break the spell and the altars that some old witch erected. Some obeah men 'plant up' the yard but you are going to go in there and root it up under Holy Ghost order. Recently I had a conversation with a beautiful woman of God. I told her that she has authority to speak a word and something happens. One day she was praying for my mom and she walked off the road and stormed into my house like a mad woman. She started ripping some things off my mom. I saw in the realms of the spirit a brown tall hair woman, grabbed a piece of stick, ran down my mother and drew a line around her. I joined the woman of God in the warfare as well and I saw my mother went 'bloop.' She was loosed. When I gave my mother the description of the person, my mom said that was her grandmother. I have never seen a picture of her.

Sometimes you start on the journey and because of the warfare and criticism you start sinking. There are some old ancestral familiar spirits that latch themselves unto you. You begin to take on the image of the family lineage. You may think I am 'coo coo' and talking non-sense? Wherever I go to preach my mom wants to accompany me. Who m the Son sets free is free indeed. Another family member would oftentimes curse the church, pastor, accusing us of worshipping the 'sun god.' She was oftentimes invited to church but she refused showing disdain for the pastor. I was persistent. When she came the pastor called and prayed for her. He discerned she needed to be loosed that very night and he encouraged the church to pray. She felt like something causing her to fall. She thought it was the pastor and insisted she will not be pushed down. But when the power of the Holy Ghost hit her she went straight to the ground. When she fell I saw a very short dwarf man, felt hat, long beard just step out of her with a puff of smoke. Yes I beheld that with my own eyes. When I told her after the service she was in utter shock. She confessed that every night as a child growing up, she saw that same man. The man would speak to her daily and meet her at a Naseberry tree. This was what bound her all of her life.

There are some things that are fighting your life that you are not aware of. When my husband was forty-four years of age the Lord revealed that the enemy wanted him dead at age forty-five. A team of us began to pray against it. He had no ailment in his body. He related that the people he grew up with had some weird beliefs and would mutter some strange things when they were going to eat. The Lord said that is the occult. He was sacrificed to die at the age of forty-five. One day before his forty-fifth birthday he was feeling ill and went to the doctor. He was diagnosed with diabetes. I told him do not accept it, tomorrow is your birthday. You are not diabetic. He ignored the warning and filled the prescription. That act of disobedience signaled his acceptance of the enemy's plan. It was set for him to die but the prayers counteracted the plans and so the enemy contrived another trick.

One day the Lord told me that he would heal my husband from what he accepted. Readers listen to me well. I knew nothing about the hair of a corn or what it can do. I do not practice herbal medicine in any way shape or form. I was about to doze off to sleep and I saw the silk of a corn. The Holy Spirit said, "Give him the hair of the corn," but I rebuked it declaring, "The blood of Jesus Christ is against you, What are you trying satan? But the Holy Spirit insisted, give it to him. I immediately researched it. Lo and behold the benefits is that it is used to treat diabetes and high blood pressure. I was flabbergasted. I shared it with someone and the person confirmed that they have used it for the same benefits and it worked.

Despite this confirmation I did not carry out the instruction. A member of the church was praying and the Lord told her that he gave me an instruction concerning my husband and I am not doing it. She said, "The Lord told you to give him the silk of the corn and he is going to heal him of diabetes." I immediately challenged her and asked if she has ever heard me speak of this. She said no. I can confirm because I did not speak of it publicly in the church. This is to corroborate that God is a God who gives revelation to build your faith in a practical way.

Confession

Sweet precious Holy Father, in the name of Jesus Christ I come before you. I acknowledge that there were times I was distracted and discouraged while you were sending the solution. I was too blinded by my pain to see it. I am sorry for discrediting you in this way. Please my Father, I ask that you release me from these sins, in Jesus precious name, Amen.

Day Four

Are You Registered?

Scripture: St. Luke 10:17 - 20

The Lord appointed seventy (70) and sent them two by two. He literally sent them on a mission and gave them instruction. But with that he gave them authority, against the kingdom of darkness, against unclean spirit, to cast out demons, heal the sick and all manner of diseases shall be healed.

Jesus knew what these seventy (70) would encounter. He acknowledged how the harvest is plenty and the labourers are few. Only a few: would stick to the mission, not get high minded, short-changed God, and take the glory for themselves. Only a few would not lose the vision of Jesus, but would keep their eyes always on him. The bible declares in Revelation 3:4, ...only a few in Sardis who have not defiled their garment.

As they returned they were focused on their accomplishments. They were moved by how the demons were subjected to them through the power of Jesus mighty name. Not understanding that at the name of Jesus every knee shall bow and every tongue shall confess that Jesus Christ is Lord. Phillipians 2:10 KJV, "*That at the name of Jesus every knee should bow, of things in heaven, and things in the earth, and things under the earth."* Even Satan knows that Jesus Christ is Lord and trembles. (James 2:19). The authority that Jesus gives in St. Luke 10:19 says, "I give unto you power to tread upon serpents and scorpions." That is not all, but overall the powers of the enemy and nothing shall by any means hurt you who carries that authority. According to St. Mark 16:18, They shall drink deadly poison and it shall not harm them. Power is given to cramp and paralyze every driving force of the enemy. We shall live by faith through the power of the living God. I implore you to learn by heart James 2:19 KJV, "*Thou believest that there is one God; thou doest well; the devils also believe, and tremble.*" Build your faith according to the confidence of this scripture and at some point in life every Christian will need this passage. Whenever there is a warfare (spiritual battle) store it up in the treasure chest of your heart, so it will be available in the hour of need.

God will use us for his glory but at no point we must get it twisted. There is danger when we get ahead of ourselves, our opponent is very cunning, he cannot defeat us, but he will labour to dullen our effectiveness, perhaps our fruitfulness as well as cutting us off from the source of power. He will cause us to be so focused on the ministry rather than the person whom we minister to.

The Lord told the disciples do not rejoice because the demons are subjected through the name of Jesus but rejoice that your **names are written in heaven**, St. Luke 10:20 KJV. If you are so busy in ministry now, it is time to get back to the power source, the real basis of your salvation (your long-term sustainability of joy). Ministry comes and goes, it has an expiry date but your relationship with the Lord Jesus Christ is forever.

Satan Fell From Glorified to Profane, Ezekiel 28:14 - 16 KJV. Satan fell from his place of authority because of his level of over-confidence. He was cut off from his power source. He thought he could operate at such high authority but he fell fast, as dramatic as lightning from heaven.

1. *From Access to heaven to restriction.* Job 1:12, I Kings 22:21, Zechariah 3:1, Rev.12:9.
2. *From the earth to bondage in the bottomless pit.* Revelation 20:1 – 3. He was cast into the pit for a thousand (1,000) years.
3. *From the pit to the lake of fire.* Revelation 20:10.

Jesus warned the disciples against pride, if Satan could fall from that place of spiritual height, status and privilege so could they in the most holy work. Pride lurks in the shadow and danger of self-glorification.

The greatest miracle one can ever see is the gift of salvation. Do not become intoxicated after a successful service or spiritual power manifesting signs and wonders but rather rejoice for the gift of salvation. (your name written in the lamb's book of life).

Confession

Oh Holy Father, you who search the deep things and know the depths of man's heart. I ask you even now that you will search my heart to the deepest place and locate any pride that is secretly hiding in me.

Lord you hate pride and the proud you see afar off. May your sword pluck it up by the seed and roots and your fire burn it to ashes. Release me from every tainting of pride in Jesus Christ Mighty name.

Day Five

The Spirit of Excellence is Upon Me

Scripture: Daniel 6

It pleased Darius the king to choose Daniel to be head over the princes because Daniel had an excellent spirit. He had a very good attitude in whatever he did and this made him the center of attention. Daniel had exceptional qualities that could not go unnoticed, so the king had no doubt that Daniel could govern the kingdom. Note what happened, because the spirit of excellence was upon him. It meant that everything which was so difficult became easy for him.

The spirit of excellence is the quality of being outstanding, it gives favour with God, (see Daniel 2:23 KJV) and with man (Daniel 2:48 KJV). God gave Daniel the interpretation of Nebuchadnezzar's dream and told him what the dream was. The magicians and astrologers were confused and confounded because they could not honour the king's command, so the king honoured Daniel. He walked with an excellent spirit so he was pre-eminent over the flesh. In this he was so yielded to the spirit of God. He allowed the spirit to lead him at all times.

Daniel's selection stirred up jealousy against him, from the 122 men that were around him. They conspired against Daniel but could find any occasion against him. He was very faithful and faultless in his character. Oftentimes when envy comes against your life, the accuser of the brethren will always look for a way to find something in your closet. If there is no weakness or sin there, he will go to great lengths to put something in the closet. These men knew Daniel well enough to know that he could not be trapped in evil. They knew he would be faithful to his God.

They studied Daniel's impeccable lifestyle and formed a conspiracy against him. As the script concluded there was no occasion found against Daniel that justified their conspiracy. He was pure and broke no law. All the counselors, governors, presidents, captain colluded to convince the king to establish a royal statute and make a firm decree that, " ..*Whosoever shall ask a petition of any God or man for thirty days, save of thee O king, he shall be cast into the den of lions*" Daniel 6:7 KJV. This decree was shrouded in deception but it appeased the king's ego and high level of pride, it speaks volumes of the king's character. The men knew that he thrived on flattery. Hence, they deceived the king to make himself a god for thirty days. Daniel's conspirators used the king's decree as a bait to entrap Daniel. He was their problem and not the king. But if they got the king, automatically they would reach the people and stir them up with hatred against Daniel.

It was such an evil and unjust behavior We must war against jealousy in prayer. It should never be taken for a candy. The moment you feel jealousy against you or against someone you must deal with it decisively and pray against it. It is highly connected to the grave and will cause evil to enter the heart of men and derail his destinies.

It was an established principle in the Media-Persian empire, that whenever a king signs and instituted a decree it was binding and not even the king himself could revoke it. When Daniel knew that the decree was signed he was confronted with a test of loyalty. Would Daniel be loyal to his king or to God? Many of us today wouldn't know how to choose, of course many may say I choose God. Yeah, sure but many of us can't choose between God and our jobs, God and our relationships, God and our worldly opportunities and God. Our sacrifice must come with a cost. It costs something to be at a higher level with God.

Daniel made a radical, permanent and very safe decision to obey God. It is always the safest decision to put yourself in trouble with man rather than God. Some people are men pleasers rather than God pleasers. The king had the power in the earth to do much harm against Daniel based on his power and authority. For example, he could make Daniel's life miserable, set up stumbling blocks, punish him, etc. Despite this, Daniel was settled in his understanding that God was completely in control. He didn't allow the decree to stop him from praying to the one true and living God. Daniel faithfully and boldly continued to pray three (3) times per day. He knew for sure that the writings were against him however, he stood for his God and he maintained his posture of prayer. His general position was that his windows were opened in his chambers, and he intentionally knelt and faced Jerusalem while he prayed.

He prayed constantly and worshipped God but he did not do it in secret. He could have compromised and closed his window when he prayed. This decree did not change his actions one way or the other, he simply continued in his excellent way of praying. He was quite cognizant of the danger of his actions. However, he exercised wisdom by not compromising his prayer by reducing or extending the time spent in his prayer session.

Daniel continued steadfastly in supplication unto his God and maintained his custom:

1. **He prayed in the upper room.** *He prayed with wisdom towards Jerusalem*, I Kings 8. Solomon asked God to give special notice, I Kings 8:30, where-ever Israel is when they prayed towards the temple in Jerusalem, God would hear and answer. `

2. **He knelt down on his knees**, mirroring Jesus' posture. "*Jesus walked on a little way before he knelt down and prayed,* (St. Luke 22:41 CEV). Likewise Stephen, Acts 7:60 KJV, Paul, (Acts 9:40 KJV) and other leaders in the church "... *we knelt on the beach and prayed.* (Acts 21:5 C.E.V). kneeling is the posture of begging and we must all come to God in this attitude reflecting the position of our heart, one of humility.

3. **He prayed three (3) times daily.** Daniel was a governor, a very busy man but that did not prevent him from finding the time to pray. He prayed and gave God thanks. When Daniel's adversaries saw him praying and giving thanks to God, it was just what they wanted to see. But for Daniel it was not just about prayer he pleaded for God's will to be accomplished. His detractors accused him of showing no regard for the king. Daniel had great respect and honour for the king but his highest respect was reserved for his God. When the king heard the words of the governors he was more displeased with himself rather than Daniel. His foolish decision has brought

harm to others.

The high cost of obedience

The king gave the command to throw Daniel into the lion's den. He had no other choice and could do nothing more to save Daniel, except to hope that Daniel's God would deliver him. Praise the name of Jesus! There is definitely no better place to have faith. The stone was sealed at the mouth of the lion's den and the king could not sleep. He rose early in the morning, went to the lion's den, and called out Daniel's name. Daniel answered with a great testimony of victory of how God sent his angel, Hebrews 1:14 KJV, to shut the lion's mouth. Daniel may have prayed according to Psalms 22:21 - 22. For he was found alone next day in the lion's den.

While Daniel knew he did nothing wrong and even declared his innocence, he was a true example of obedience. And he truly believed in his God although they wanted him to look disobedient. He was preserved through faith and kept from the paws and the jaws of the lions by the power of God.

The fate of those who plotted against Daniel including their wives and children had a devastating end. They were thrown in the den where the lions overpowered them before they reached the bottom. They all perished in the destructive trap they set for Daniel as declared in Psalm 7:14 - 16. Daniel's obedience almost cost him his life. Your life may be required for your obedience to God. Daniel was victorious in this warfare as a result of his unwavering faith in God, and sustaining an excellent spirit.

Confession

Heavenly Father, excellent God in all your ways. As your precious little child I come to you in confidence. I now ask you Father, to forgive me for the times I allowed provocations and insults to distract me from my steadfastness in prayer like Daniel. Oh God, I ask that you purify me and give me your grace and an excellent spirit to be resolute and never deny you, even in the lion's den.

Day Six

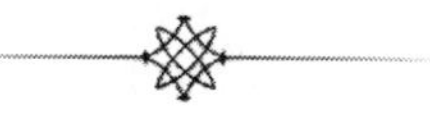

Face To Face with My Lord

Scripture: Exodus 33

The people watched Moses and they noticed that as Moses worshipped they worshipped also. This prompted the people to draw closer to God by this example. Moses' tent did not become the tabernacle of meetings because he called it so, but because God's presence met him there, in the pillar of cloud. The pillar of cloud was tangible and vivid as it stood at the door of Moses' tent. This was a good example and the people were strengthened because they were confident with the fact that their leader met with God. It flows natural to live by this example of Moses. Numbers 12:8, CEV "*...With him will I speak mouth to mouth even is then were ye not afraid to speak against my servant Moses?*" God spoke to Moses face to face, he heard clearly and plainly from God, other prophets heard in dreams and visions. Moses and God had a free and opened fellowship. Moses had a personal revival with God and this was a special example to the nation of Israel and Joshua, Joshua did not depart from the temple. The more Moses drew closer to God it also drew Joshua close to God.

Moses said to God you have not let me know who you will send with me. Moses was determined to have God's presence with Him even though God told him before that he would send an angel with him, Genesis 33:13 KJV. Moses made a request, if I found grace in your sight at this point I am feeling that Moses had a little obsession with God. The Psalmist said, "In his presence there is fullness of joy and at his right hand there are pleasures forever more." (Psalm 16:11 KJV). The more of God Moses received the more he needed. He was in the earth but connected everything to God in heaven. This is having pre-eminence over the flesh.

God gave Moses his heart's desire but Moses continued to press God for more affirmation of his promise. God told him, my presence will go with you and I will give you rest. This presence is the angel of God a full manifestation of God. Exodus 23:20 KJV, "*Behold, I send an angel before thee, to keep thee in the way, and to bring thee into the place which I have prepared.*" God's presence means rest. He is far above principalities and powers. No driving force of evil can conquer you when you have the presence of the Lord.

Moses was so bold and confident in his conversations with God, he cautioned God of the consequences of not keeping his promise, (see Genesis 33:15). He vehemently declared! "Do not carry us up if you are not coming, if you are not with us, we will not go!" Moses wanted something special for Israel, to show that they were not like the other nations. They had the unique presence of God's power going with them. Try to understand that when God is with you, your generation/nation will be different because of your excellent way.

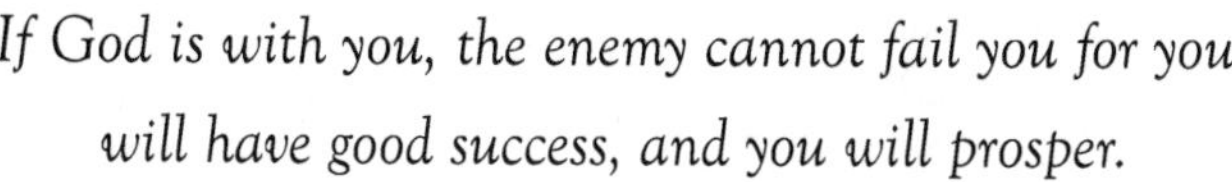

If God is with you, the enemy cannot fail you for you will have good success, and you will prosper.

Apostle Dr. Nichole Masters

According to Joshua 1:8; God told Joshua that the book of the law, should be meditated on day and night for good success. Moses wanted something extra from God, based on his concern he asked, *"How are the other nations different from us and how do we know that we are really your people?"*

1. They are looking on at us
2. They are laughing at us
3. They are mocking and jeering us

God we want to be seen as a separated and unique people. God assured him that he will do this thing that Moses asked. God answered his intercession and Moses found grace in the sight of the Lord his God. God displayed his presence to Moses. Moses encountered his goodness, God did not show him his justice, power or wrath against sin. All these aspects are really God's true nature but what he displayed to Moses was pure love, goodness and mercy. Moses' determination pulled God's presence to a life changing encounter like never before. It was an encounter that brought him face to face with God which in turn gave Moses confidence, boldness and power for his journey.

Confession

Father, in the name of Jesus I come to you today. Forgive me of all the things I have done wrong, wash me, cleanse me, forgive me, Lord help me to be sold out to you, give me power over my flesh. Help all my desires to be on you. Let your goodness, mercies and grace be my portion perpetually.

Day Seven

Put Me in The Cleft of The Rock: (Show Me Your Glory Lord)

Scripture: Exodus 33; Hebrews 11

I beseech you oh Lord show me thy glory. Do you understand the humble desperation of Moses with his request? I believe this posture of prayer has to reach into a stimulated dimension in the realms (of the spirit), for Moses to acquire this level of knowledge and take this bold step. Moses received his God given rights. Moses won a yes answer from God, when he asked for the special presence of God to remain with Israel for their journey to the promised land, *Exodus 33:12 – 17* KJV.

He also won a confirmation of the promise from God and an affirmation of a close relationship. This was similar to Peter on the Mount of transfiguration when he asked for something not really understanding what he said. Indeed a bold request yet God granted it. This is a true sign of revival in the heart of Moses. What about you today? Are you longing for a revival? Moses was like David who declared, *as the Deer panteth after the water brooks, so panteth my soul after you oh God, Psalm 42:1KJV.*

Moses had an insatiable appetite for the presence of God. The more he received was the more he desired. He must have spent some quality time with God. Everything in him must be praising and clamouring, he longed to know the Lord in a more deeper and genuine way. A mark of true revival was indeed upon him. And when there is revival there is also restoration. He wanted more and more of God. The more a man knows of God is the more he is desirous of knowing him.

You may be a Christian who is saved for many years, or a new convert. But have you really longed for more of God's direct presence? An encounter with God or his direct presence? Of course you pray and fast but that is not the concern. Have you consulted God about his desires not wavering or unmovable but steadfastly, intentionally, and I daresay chronically? **Show me your glory** - takes me a step higher, draw me closer to thee oh Lord. **Show me your glory** – more and more Moses needed God.

Exodus 16:10 KJV, *And it came to pass as Aaron spake unto the whole congregation of the children of Israel, that they looked toward the wilderness, and behold the glory of the LORD appeared in the cloud."* As Aaron instructed Israel they looked towards the wilderness and saw the glory of the Lord. Also in Exodus 24:16 – 17 KJV, [16]*and the glory of the LORD abode upon mount Sinai and the cloud covered it six days and the seventh day he called unto Moses out of the midst of the cloud.* [17]*and the sight of the glory of the Lord was like devouring fire on the top of the mount in the eyes of the children of Israel.* The glory of the Lord rested on Mount Sinai and the cloud covered it 6 days. The consuming fire of God was on top of the mountain in the eyes of the children of Israel. How he wanted to see the Ka'bod – the manifested glory of God (weight of

God).

Show me your glory – God said to Moses I cannot show you my face but I will show you my glory, his grace and his goodness. God could not show Moses his face, no man at any time can see the face of God and live. God called Moses to a new place and position where he would meet him. So he instructed Moses to go stand in a specific place (later Elijah met God in that very place, I Kings 19:8 – 18). God's glory passed by Moses, and he had to cover Moses with his hands as he passed.

Are you longing to hear God telling you, there is a place by me that you must go? There is something more I want to do with you? The songwriter concurred, Rock of Ages cleft for me, let me hide myself in thee. This is God's protection. Show me your glory Lord.

Isaiah encountered God's glory, Isaiah 6 and it moved him to grieve his sins and unworthiness. John experienced some of God's glory and fell at the feet of Jesus like a dead man, Rev.1:17 KJV. Paul experienced God's glory on the way to Damascus but he could barely describe it, 2 Corinthians 12. Moses could only see God's back part, (not his full glory) just the after effect of his radiant glory that had just passed. God showed Moses only what he could bear and see not as he desired. God has a great sense of humour.

When God draws near He:

- Gives revelation – supernaturally blesses and gives protection. He grants desires, this is a true demonstration that God rewards every heart that seeks him, 2 Cor. 3:18 KJV, But we all, with open face *beholding as in a glass, the glory of the Lord, are changed into the same image from glory to glory, even as by the spirit of the Lord. May the glory to glory be your portion. May the mirror of his glory brings transformation by the spirit of the Lord upon your life as you seek him in this season.*

Confession

Father I come before you this day, I thank you for your grace and your mercies, blot out All my transgression, forgive me of all my sins, lead me into the place of total victory. Bestow your blessings upon me this day, let nothing in me hinder your blessing. Lord, search me, try me, purge me and free me in Jesus Mighty name.

Day Eight

My Cup of Victory

Scripture: Numbers 22

Israel was at this point on the move, they had completed 40 years exile in the wilderness. As they set forward they advanced towards Moab, along the Jordan. Now Moab was afraid because of the children of Israel. They were very many and they were victorious over neighbouring nations. Balak's fear caused by the intimidation of Israel may seem plausible. However, if he had believed God then he would have nothing to fear. God did not want Israel to have that land and so Israel would not need to trouble Moab, Deut. 2:9 KJV, "*And the LORD said unto me, distress not the Moabites, neither contend with them in battle: for I will not give thee of their land for a possession, because I have given Are unto the children of Lot for a possession.*" Balak sent to a man called Balaam. He was not an Israelite but he came to some knowledge of the true God. He was not a prophet of God, he was a pagan from a foreign nationality. He believed he had a way with the gods.

Because Balak was fearful of Israel he called for the response team of hell, Balaam the diviner, to curse the blessed ones. He felt threatened because of Israel's continued victory. This is how a lot of people are. Sometimes warfare comes to you because you live on victory street, prosperity boulevard and success is in your DNA. They will work over-time to take you out of your privileged place of victory. But stand firm with confidence knowing God is in control.

Balaam was able to give a full discourse of the background of Israel. They were a set of people who covered the entire region, they abide against me, therefore come and lay a curse on them. My friend, witchcraft is real but let not your heart be troubled, if God be for you then who can be against you?

Balak wanted Balaam to cripple Israel spiritually, so they could be defeated in battle. The devil knows who you are. He knows the source of your strength and your capabilities. Stand firm on your most holy faith and fight from a place of victory. The devil is like a roaring lion seeking whom to devour. Historically, it seemed as if Balaam was renowned as a mighty man of spiritual things. As far as Balak was concerned whenever Balaam blessed a man he was blessed and whenever he cursed a man he was cursed. The messengers persuaded Balaam to give a diviner's fee against Israel. Balaam invited the men to lodge at his place for the night, so he could hear from God regarding his offer. His true heart was revealed, he was a man with super-natural gift but not a genuine heart after God. He was seeking God's will regarding something that was clearly not God's will. He was controlled by the spirit of mammon. He loved money and tried to manipulate God into granting him a special exception.

God visited Balaam and asked him a question, Who are those men with you? God already knew the answer but Balaam was naïve, and in ignorance of these men's evil intention. The Lord instructed Balaam, "D*o not go, and do not curse these people because they are blessed.*" He rose up in the morning and told his guests to return to their land without him because the Lord refused to grant him permission. Of course Balak wasn't pleased and so he sent more of his men again. This time of a higher rank and a greater reward. The demand was great, it was not just the diviner's fee that Balaam stood to gain but great wealth. This tantalized the avaricious appetite of Balaam. He was under God's conviction and responded, "*...I cannot go beyond the word of my God to do less or more." Numbers 22:18 KJV.*

Balaam's words confirmed the reality that he had an encounter with God; although he wanted to honour Balak's request. His heart was set on the money but, '*who God bless no man curse.*' God revealed himself to a pagan diviner just for his people. Once again Balaam told the messengers to stay where they were while he seek the Lord a second time. Of a fact, he was only entertaining the sin of lust and entice for money. He already got the revelation from Numbers 22:12 KJV and needed no further clarification. He used words that seem spiritual and godly, "Let me seek the Lord about this." God's words can never change. Balaam constantly provoked the Lord and so the Lord told him to get up and go but only speak what he permitted, Numbers 22:20 KJV, *And God came unto Balaam at night, and said unto him if the men come to call thee, rise up and go with them but yet the word which I shall say unto thee that shalt thou do.* Sometimes God says no to the prayers of his people, because of his love but sometimes God says yes to the desires of the wicked for he will judge them.

God's anger was aroused against Balaam because he went. He rejected God's voice of command spoken through his conscience.

God had every reason to be angry.

The angel of the Lord took a stand against the stubbornness of Balaam because of his greed. The anger of the Lord blocked the path as he rode on his donkey. At this point Balaam did not see the angel. The dust of covetousness was upon his eyes and it dazzled with the glitter of fake promotion.

The donkey saw the angel of the Lord. I dare say the dumb ass was more spiritual. The prophet had a spiritual gift but a disobedient heart and life. (a blind seer seeing less than a dumb animal). The donkey responded in obedience as he turned aside and away from the disaster. It sat down to avoid judgment. This caused the disobedient prophet's foot to be crushed against the wall. The stiff-necked prophet suffered and caused his animal to suffer too. He struck the ass several times, the Lord gave the dumb ass speech. It spoke to Balaam and rebuked his master. Balaam's anger boiled against the donkey and he wanted to kill it. "*Good people are kind to their animals but a mean person is cruel*," Proverbs 12:10 CEV. Balaam had to humble himself before the donkey because this was not the natural behavior of the faithful donkey.

God rebuked Balaam and told him that his ways were perverse. His small idea of repentance brought him to the place of admitting he has sinned as the angel of the Lord stood with a drawn sword in his hand. Balaam's ways displeased God, "*Which have forsaken the right way, and are gone astray, following the way of Balaam the son of Bosor, who loved the wages of unrighteousness,*" (2 Peter 2:15). Balaam's sin was the love for money, "[11]*Now they are in for real trouble. They have followed Cain's example and have made the same mistake that Balaam did by caring only for money. They have also rebelled against God, just as Korah did Because of all this, they will be destroyed," Jude 1:11 NLT.*

He was willing to disobey God and to curse God's people for money. God gave Balaam over to his sinful desires, (Romans 1:24 - 28). Sometimes God gives over man to their desires of sin. Sin is destructive, so if God gives you over to your desires what shall be your end? Self-destruction will be the ultimate end.

Confession

Father, I thank you for the gift of the Holy Spirit which is my conscience and guide. Oh Lord, please forgive me of all the times that I was stiff necked like Balaam. Lord Jesus I ask that you wash my eyes, with eye salve that I will clearly see dangers and avoid walking in them.

Day Nine

Don't Run, It Is Time to Answer the Call

Scripture: Jonah 1:3 – 17

God spoke to Jonah the son of Amittai concerning Nineveh. It was a great city but it was full of wickedness which went up before God. He planned to destroy Nineveh according to their wickedness. Scriptures are filled with examples that God will not destroy a city without a warning (Ezekiel 33:4 - 5, Jeremiah 4:20, Ezekiel 3:7). The Lord spoke to Jonah in a powerful way. He gave him two (2) instructions:

1. *"Go to Nineveh the great city (capital of the Assyrian empire).* It was huge and prominent but it was not a city of Israel. It belonged to the pagans and Gentiles. God called them to repentance. The warning and judgment of God was upon them. But Jonah rose up and fled, he was a reluctant prophet. Or may be Jonah saw it as a difficult task. Based on the history of the people he saw it as an impossible mission.

2. *"Preach against it, because their wickedness has come up against me."Jonah 3:1 KJV. Nahum 3:1* – 4, gave a good idea of how wicked the people were. "[1]*Doom to the crime capital! Nineveh,*

city of murder and treachery. [2] *Here is your fate – cracking whips, churning wheels; galloping horses, roaring chariots,* [3] *cavalry attacking, swords and spears flashing; soldiers stumbling over piles of dead bodies.* [4] *You were nothing more than a prostitute using your magical charms and witchcraft to attract and trap nations."* It could be Jonah thought that he would be mocked and treated as a fool because of their power and authority. Sometimes when you look at society and how advanced they are in sin, the truth be told the gospel looks like foolishness.

Another of Jonah's concerns could be, he thought he would be killed if he did what the Lord told him to do. He probably thought the Assyrians in Nineveh could escape God's judgment. St. Matthew 28:19 – 20 instructs that, the Lord's disciples should go into all the nations of the world and make disciples.

Jonah ran or should I say fled from the presence of God and went to Tarshish. He went far away from Nineveh. He paid his money and went on a ship – a dangerous impulse, a brave one drove Jonah there but it was wrong. Jonah should have read Psalm 139:7 – 10, and he would have understood that he cannot hide from God. You can't escape the presence of God.

God prevented Jonah's escape he sent a storm. The storm was so strong, enough to break up the ship which put the vessel and the sailors into a dangerous place. Jonah endangered the entire ship. The sailors of the ship sought their superstitious god. These men began to throw out their cargo, in a bid to lighten the ship and call upon the name of their false god to enquire what was the reason for their calamity.

Meanwhile, Jonah was comfortable in the bottom of the ship, fast asleep while the storm raged. Some of us prophets are sleeping while the storm is raging. Jonah slept as a careless Christian sleeps. He slept while a prayer meeting was going on, although it was prayer to a false god. There is a marked difference between the sleeping and fully awakened Christian.

The Sleeping Christians:

1. Sleeping Christians do not like prayer meetings.
2. Sleeping Christians are really clueless as to what is going on.
3. Jonah slept while the heathen needed him.
4. Sleeping Christians snooze on while the world needs their messages and testimonies.

The Christian who is fully awakened

1. Is fully awakened to the spirit of God.
2. Has thorough consciousness of the reality of spiritual things.
3. Does not take the Son of God to be a fancy, heaven to be a fiction or hell to be a tale.

The captain realized that Jonah was sleeping, Arise you sleeper! The soldiers discovered that Jonah was the source of the problem as the lot fell on him. They began to ask questions:

1. What is your occupation? He answered I am a prophet. 2 Kings 14:25 KJV, "*.....according to the word of the LORD God of Israel, which he spake by the hand of Jonah, the son of Amittai, the*

prophet, which was of Gathepher." proved that Jonah was a recognized prophet. Jonah knew the truth about God. His claim to fear is only true because he was running away from God.

2. Why have you done this? The unbelievers rebuked Jonah. At his own request he asked to be thrown off the ship into the sea. The sea was tempestuous. They rowed very hard to reach dry land as they feared God, and moreover to throw a prophet in the sea. The sea became more boisterous and so they prayed then throw Jonah over board. Immediately the sea ceased its raging.

Jonah in the fish's belly

The Lord prepared a great fish to swallow Jonah just because he was disobedient. Jonah had his regrets but in the fish's belly he cried unto the Lord by reason of his affliction. The Lord heard him from out of the fish's belly and answered.

Confession

Heavenly Father, mighty deliverer I come to you today. I bear my soul to you as nothing is hidden from you. Your words declare obedience is better than sacrifice. Oh Father, I am guilty at times when I run away from my assignment like Jonah did, because of the warfare and battles. In this I have sinned. Oh Lord, please forgive me, purge me and loose me and set me free from every seed of disobedience.

Day Ten

There Is a Fourth Man in The Fire

Scripture: Daniel 3

The instruction was given to gather together the satraps – a Persian word that means protector of the realms (a specific category of public officials). The officials of the province were invited to the dedication of an image as a test of allegiance. There was a command given to worship the image and whomever did not worship the image would be penalized. This was backed by a powerful threat from king Nebuchadnezzar. Refusal to worship the image was treason, not only a religious offense but it was tied to both political and spiritual allegiance.

Nebuchadnezzar was not a man who allowed law-breakers to go unpunished. He was described as a person devoted to justice, he did not rest night or day. The crowd was committed to the king's command except these three young men (Shadrach, Meshach and Abednego). Nebuchadnezzar's grand idolatry was accompanied by music. The Hebrew boys refused to bow, Daniel 3:12, and were accused by the Chaldeans. The Chaldeans had an obvious political motivation against the Jews who were promoted to high offices along with Daniel in the events recorded in the previous chapter.

Note, you will not be able to go through life without being discovered. A lighted candle cannot be hidden. Hiding your light under a bushel is an intention to stay low during the war time and emerge when the palms are being distributed. You hope to enter by the back lanes.

The king enquired, "Is it true?" He wanted to hear what the Hebrew boys had to say. Is it necessary for a man to profess to be what he is not? Can you be true to Christ even when facing fear? Just imagine the pressure upon these young men? The king, the furnace, the compatriots, their competitors. All of this conspiracy was to convince them to compromise.

But I want to say to someone today, do not judge the situation by the king's threat nor the heat that is coming from the furnace, but by the everlasting God and the everlasting promise that await you. These men of God were resolute! They decided they will not worship the image. They had no need to answer in that matter. They boldly declared, "Our God that we serve is able to deliver." They were confident that God could save them from both fire and king. But if not – they had the understanding and submission to God. They knew God's power but they also knew they had to do the right thing, even if God does not show up.

They did not doubt God's ability but neither did they pressure to know God's will. In this way they agreed with Job 13:15, though he slay me yet will I trust him. They fully embraced, I John 2:15 KJV, *"Love not the world, neither the things that are in the world, if any man loves the world the love of the Father is not in him."*

In the past they were challenged to eat impure food, they refused and God blessed their obedience. Many failed in their obedience because they went for something big to test their faith before they really start to obey. Some compromise, while there are some who will stand firm.

In Daniel 3:24, the king was astonished when he heard the Hebrew boys giving praise and worship like Paul and Silas in Acts 16:25 KJV, "*At midnight Paul and Silas prayed and sang praises unto God, and the prisoners heard them.*" Jesus was literally watching them in the midst of their worst trials. In every fiery situation Jesus will always be there as the fourth man in the fire. What are your circumstances today? What are you facing? What is it that the enemy has conspired against you?

Nebuchadnezzar was astonished when he saw that those on the outside perished while those thrown in the fire had peace, in the midst of it. Nebuchadnezzar described the fourth person in the fire as the *Son of God.* Jesus was definitely with them and it could be seen.

God's people are always in furnaced positions. They may be different in nature but are similar by their purpose in this life. Whatever furnace that is prepared by man or by God, always remember that God is a deliverer and he will always deliver us miraculously. He will sustain and give us perpetual strength. Even in the strongest trials.

Confession

Lord Jesus, great and terrible God, I come to you today, just as I am. Today I ask that you give me the strength to endure the furnace of life's journey. Give me stability to stand with you and for you in loyalty. Confidently standing in the line of fire but resulting in victory in Jesus mighty name. Heavenly father, forgive me for every time I stand in doubt, not understanding my journey. Thank you for your grace and new mercies in Jesus mighty name, Amen.

Day Eleven

Every High Thing Must Come Down – I

Scripture: Daniel 4:1 - 18

Nebuchadnezzar was a Gentile King who was also recognized as a great king as he had a great kingdom that the Lord had given him until he got corrupted, so as per usual, Satan always wants the glory. The fact that Nebuchadnezzar stood to challenge God, He made an example out of him. Daniel 4:4, introduces the pompous demeanor of Nebuchadnezzar, "*I Nebuchadnezzar was at rest in mine house, and flourishing in my palace.*" This of course was a false sense of security and his peace was also false. The peace of this world can never be true and is temporary peace, not from God but from his own confidence.

Nebuchadnezzar had a very disturbing dream where he called for all his wise men, magicians, astrologers, but they could not interpret the dream. He sent for Daniel as a last resort which was a graceless behavior. That is how it is, graceless people always sees God's people as last resort and that is the sad truth. The king saw in his dream a great tree, noticing everything about it from size, strength, prominence, beauty, fruit and shelter. Although the tree was poised with all its grandeur its fate was doom as It would be chopped down, eradicating its magnificence. Another important point to note is that the tree was symbolic of a man who would be transformed and given the heart of a beast. The transformation of the tree was that it would no longer be free and great but bound with a band of iron and bronze. This example of this great tree was for man to see God as Sovereign and not Nebuchadnezzar.

Nebuchadnezzar heard these words in his dream as it was a very detailed dream and would not have been hard to interpret, and clearly dealing with the humbling of a great King. Maybe his counselors knew what it meant but were scared to tell him the interpretation. Nebuchadnezzar's pride was so high that it distanced him from even a speck of humility. It is a natural thing with man that when pride is high he will never take correction, and that is a very bad state to be in. like Lucifer, he lifted up himself before the Almighty God, in that, the King gave glory to himself instead of God. It was all about the I, (the ego), for the King, as in the case of most ancient and modern authority figures – Nebuchadnezzar wanted to believe that he ruled instead of God or anyone else. But every high thing must come down.

Daniel gave the interpretation of the dream without compromising, therefore Nebuchadnezzar recognized that Daniel was different from all the other men and the king addressed them as such. He knew that Daniel would be honest enough to give all the interpretation, and the King's commendation of Daniel conveyed a significant message of his steadfastness to God in Babylon. "You are able and the spirit of the Holy God is upon you." Despite acknowledging Daniel's God, that didn't bring conviction upon him to surrender to the all-powerful God.

God loves his people, even when we are not deserving of his love. He is a jealous God and he will break us to make us humble. Humility is the honest recognition of our own worth, based on how God sees us and not how we see ourselves or the world sees us. There is also a delicate balance between humbly recognizing our sin, yet knowing how much God loves and values us. Pride elevates us above others and even above God himself and results in degrading our sense of self-worth. Walking in pride is repulsive to God because it denies the true value that God placed upon us, when He created us in his own image. We must always strive to see ourselves as God sees us and that must be our original goal.

What about you today? Are you too high for the gospel, the church, the Holy Spirit and the things concerning the Lord Jesus Christ? Where are you today? Is God pleased with your present posture? This tree that Nebuchadnezzar saw in his dream was flourishing, great and productive but all was wasted. Although it demonstrated greatness it wasn't good as pride stained every bark and every leaf, and God had no choice but to cut it down. Every high thing must come down!

Confession

Great and terrible God, as I come before you, I humble myself in your very presence. Lord I now ask you to take me to a humble place continually. Oh Lord help me to be the best me according to your divine place for my life. Today I sit in the seat of a child and now ask that you be seen in every area and circumstances of my life, in Jesus mighty name, Amen.

Day Twelve

From Casting Down to a Great Rising

Scripture: Daniel 4:1 – 19; 37

Daniel genuinely cared for King Nebuchadnezzar. He was astonished at the dream and the whole thing troubled him. Great men and prophets are oftentimes represented as trees, (see Ezekiel 17:6 and Psalm 1:3). Daniel explained the dream to Nebuchadnezzar, maybe the King could not wrap the interpretation around his finger and how it would be fulfilled, but God had spoken. There are some persons at times who try to reason out the move and mind of God, and they fail to recognize that it is more about what God said about the matter. God's intention was really for the King to avoid the humiliation, God wanted him to humble himself.

The king was positioned in a mighty way and very high where his height reached to the sky. His leaves as depicted in the dream were great and special, so vast bearing abundant fruit. It had much meat, the fowls of the air would depend on it, the beast of the field would cling to it. The king had grown and become mighty, powerfully dominating the earth and forgetting that he was mere mortal and so he did not humble himself and repent. If he had emulated Jonah (see

Jonah 3), he would have definitely risen from the great fall. At the end of twelve (12) months, God gave the King grace, but he disgraced the grace.

During the 7 years of exile from human civilization, the arm of insanity was upon the king. He began to think like animals and also imitated their behaviour, and therefore could not function like a man. Although he was given the opportunity to humble himself before God he did not, so God had to do the humbling himself. Nebuchadnezzar could only see the truth about himself only when he saw the truth about God therefore the King learnt his lesson in the worst possible way.

In order to get the King to a low place God had to cut him down and as such, those who walk in pride will be cut to an unknown place. Know that God resists the proud but gives grace to the humble. James 4:16 TMSG, *"As it is, you are full of your grandiose self, all such vaunting, self-importance is evil."* Pride is number one on God's most hated list of sins, Proverbs 6:16 - 19 NIV, [16] How much better to get wisdom rather than gold, to get insight rather than silver! [17] The highway of the upright avoids evil; those who guard their ways preserve their lives. [18] Pride goes before destruction, a haughty spirit before a fall. [19] Better to be lowly in spirit along with the oppressed than to share plunder with the proud.

Nebuchadnezzar's story will prove that God will glorify himself in the nations. Here he took some of the treasures of the Jerusalem temple and placed them in the temple of his gods, and he had false reasons to believe that his gods were stronger than the Most High God of Abraham. Indeed he was too high! Let us not forget who God is in our lives and the expectation of God's purpose in our lives. Even when you are cut down for your pride if you humble yourself, God

Will lift you up to a great rising.

Confession

Almighty Everlasting Father, I come before you with my heart broken and contrite. Lord I ask you to keep my heart from being lifted up in pride. Your words declare that the proud you see a far off. Lord I ask for your humility and grace to remain in your presence, in Jesus name amen.

Day Thirteen

Defilement Comes from Within and not Without

Scripture: St. Matthew 15:1 - 16

If a man eats the most bizarre thing he cannot be defiled based on what went into his body; but what comes out of a man is what brings defilement upon the man. St. Matthew 15:11 KJV, "*Not that which goeth into the mouth defileth a man; but that which cometh out of the mouth, this defileth the man.*" These scribes and Pharisees were at Jerusalem and they came to accuse Jesus because of his ministry. Noticing that the disciples paid no attention to their tradition of washing hands before eating bread, they found it fit to accuse Jesus and His disciples saying that they are not living a righteous life.

They then approached Jesus for an explanation as to why His disciples seemingly disregarded their tradition. They exclaimed, "How can they be teaching the word of God and at the same time they are not washing their hands before eating bread?" Jesus did in fact reply to them. Their complaint was that the disciples transgressed against the tradition of the elders, and in their estimation they thought that they asked Jesus a pertinent question. What I love about Jesus is that

He is the Word and he can never be twisted.

Once these hypocrites would come to Jesus they would come based on Moses' law. Jesus did not come to change the law but as the fulfillment of the law as He was above the level of their hypocrisy, traditions and religiosity; and He came to correct some things. He came to correct the essence and the true value of salvation, the church and of who Jesus was and is; while these Scribes and Pharisees paid no attention to it because they were more religious. It is therefore clear that man who is religious denies the power and effect of the living God.

Jesus in return spake back to them and asked, "Why do you transgress against the commandments of God by your tradition?" These people thought that the disciples were offending and sinning against the elders of the land. Jesus went in and showed another picture of who is in the trouble with his thought provoking question, that exposed who was really sinning against the commandments of God. The commandment of God says, "v6...*Honour your father and mother and do not curse them and you show no regard for this,*" and this was a bone of contention for them. The bible declares that just as Isaiah addressed the hypocrisy of the people, so Jesus addressed these modern hypocrites with that scripture, Isaiah 29:13 KJV, "*Wherefore the Lord said, forasmuch as this people draw near me with their mouth, and with their lips do honour me, but have removed their heart far from me and their fear towards me is taught by the precept of man.*"

Even those persons who thought they were in a good state by tradition and religiosity, the bible declares that all of what they did was lip service, as they had no connection or relationship with God and were more caught up in tradition. Sadly, many of us in Christendom are caught up in tradition, but the way of the Lord is not in us. But what is God saying about our lives? What direction and instruction is God giving us?

Personally in my earlier years of going to church, in the New Testament body, I would not wear earrings or bracelets, and I would comb my hair in a particular way. This was based on our tradition, I thought christians going to church and wearing earrings or any form of jewelry were sinning against God but by the time I left the church I would put on back my ornaments. It is funny how today if I walk in any New Testament church I can put on my earring, make-up and ornaments with modesty and no one would have an issue. My earlier concept of Christianity saw me equating modesty to wearing the tallest dress and the oldest piece of garment, but that was pure religiosity, a lie from the pit of hell!

Many of us today are of the opinion that our tradition dictates how we serve God; and the Word declares that God is a spirit and they that worship him must worship him in spirit and in truth (St. John 4:24 KJV). These people worshipped God in vain, in other words, they are just being 'mout a massi' (chatterbox). St. Matthew 15:9 KJV echoes that, "*But in vain they do worship me teaching for doctrines the commandments of man.*" They take away from the whole purpose of salvation and now they teach in a condemning way because of their tradition. They no longer look at the heart, but at rituals and dictate that this is how you serve God, and Jesus had to address this error.

When you look at certain religions and the things they practise you realize that it is merely tradition they engage in. For example, some think that in order to worship their god they have to be fully cladded in clothing, except for their eyes, especially the women; where some would be in black and white and only their eyes were left uncovered. So in essence, they serve God in bondage based on tradition, but if you check the heart it is far from the true and living God. In other religions the men wear some garments from their head to their feet with a little hat on the head, and this is how they traditionally serve God. Therefore, once you are connected to this group you are subjected to the one order, but it has nothing to do with the heart.

Others pray three times per day but it is ritualistic and has nothing to do with the power, dunamis, effectiveness of reaching to God. They would bow with their religiosity but their heart was not being touched in any shape or form. You would find others abstaining from certain foods, meats, and they would not see the real evidence of serving Almighty God. Understand that certain rituals in the worship service take away from the Holy Spirit of the living God therefore preventing a move of God.

I want to caution you, that you cannot serve God by tradition. Jesus said, "*By your tradition you make the word of God of non-effect.*" The word of God declares that "*The Word is quick and powerful and sharper than any two edged sword, it cuts, divides and put asunder where bones and marrow meet* (Hebrews 4:12 KJV). So traditions and rituals make the word of God of no effect. Jesus would always have a bone to pick with the Scribes and Pharisees because he came to shed light; but when Jesus spoke to them, the disciples realized that they were offended by the sayings of Jesus Christ. The bible declares that the Word of God is a stumbling block to a man who is wicked (see I Peter 2:8)

"St. John 8:12 declares that, "*He came as a light to a dark world,*" Other scriptures outline that Jesus came to root up, pluck up, tear down and destroy the kingdom of darkness, (Jeremiah 1:10). He did not come with false peace, but with the sword to cut off the foreskin of men and to stir them.

(Deuteronomy, 10:6 KJV) But they lift their heart against Jesus and conspired to get rid of Him in the earth, not realizing that by defending their tradition they were allowing the scriptures to be fulfilled. The bible declares that He was wounded for our transgression, He was bruised for our iniquities; the chastisement of our peace was upon him and by his stripes we are delivered and set free (Isaiah 53:5).

John the Baptist the fore runner of Jesus Christ was baptizing, and when he looked he saw Jesus coming and he declared, "Behold the lamb of God whose shoe latchet I am not worthy to unloose," (St. John 1:29). Jesus went to him and asked him to baptize him, but John was awestruck as he looked at his unworthiness in comparison to Jesus. "I am not worthy to pull your shoes but here you come to me to be baptized" John said; but Jesus responded, "It was so that the scriptures can be fulfilled." Glory be to God, understand that many things happened in scriptures mainly for the scriptures to be fulfilled.

Jesus died for man's redemption., so that we could have life in abundance, therefore the effectiveness of the Word must be among us and not by tradition. The mandate of God is to cut off the life support of eternal damnation, and to give us eternity with Jesus Christ and this must be established in the earth. I would like to caution us to pay no attention to tradition, as this cannot get you to heaven or allow you to walk the walk that Jesus called us to walk in this earth. We do not serve God by tradition but by commandment and by His word. The Scribes and Pharisees were offended and the disciples acknowledged that.

Jesus said to the disciples, "anything that my Father did not plant it shall be uprooted." There are some things that are happening that Jesus Christ did not plant, so once God did not plant it, it must and shall be uprooted. Isaiah 9:15 – 16 reads, [15] "*The ancient and honourable, he is the head; and the prophet that teacheth lies, he is the tail.* [16] *For the leaders of this people cause them to err; and they that are led of them are destroyed.*" So I re-iterate that anything God did not plant shall be uprooted.

Now appreciate that there are some leaders that God did not plant. The bible said that the honourable operate at the head but the prophet that preacheth lies, operate at the tail. Consequently, some leaders are operating from the position of the tail and have caused God's people to sin, and further operating in error because of their blindness. Because these men are blind and the people whom they lead are blind the bible said they caused them also to be destroyed, and to buttress this point, St. Matthew 15:14 KJV outlines, "*Let them alone: they be blind leaders of the blind. And if the blind lead the blind, both shall fall into the ditch.*"

Jesus saw them as blind leaders leading a blind set of people, that's why when we serve God by tradition based on what our leaders and the heads of the churches are saying and it has no biblical base, it is of no effect. When Jesus said these things Peter did not understand what he was saying, accordingly, he asked Jesus to explain the parable. Jesus asked him, "Are you also without understanding?" Although Peter was around Jesus he did not always understand him because he was not in the spirit most of the time; and was limited in his understanding and revelation. Jesus challenged Peter with the question for him to see if he too was operating as a blind person.

Jesus brought clarity with St. Matthew 5:17 KJV, "*Do not ye yet understand, that whatsoever entereth in at the mouth goeth into the belly, and is cast out into the draught?*" In essence Jesus was saying to Peter that whatever you eat by the mouth it goes into the belly and then exit the body as waste. It will provide nutrient to the muscles, tissues and other organs and cells but it will not stay inside of the man. But St. Matthew 15:18 KJV drives home Jesus point extrapolating "*But those things which proceed out of the mouth come forth from the heart; and they defile the man.*" Jesus clarity was not only to the Scribes, Pharisees and Peter but to even us today.

It cannot be over emphasized that whatever goes in a man through the mouth it cannot bring defilement; but what makes a man unclean, is the evil that proceeds out of the abundance of the heart. When evil is in the heart it is going to manifest one way or another, so what comes out of the man makes him unclean. Of course these Scribes and Pharisees were guilty of all these things, yet they sought to accuse and judge Jesus' disciples, or rather condemn them because they did not wash their hands when they ate.

How many of us are guilty of these things today? Some are guilty because they do not wear a hat to church, but those who wear hats to church are in the bed of fornication, adultery, murder, slander all kinds of immoral situations. Let us draw near to the Lord Jesus Christ by the power of his word and destroy the power of tradition that seeks to dominate salvation. Jesus died for man's redemption, and that we can have eternal life with Christ our heavenly father. His words declare that I am gone to prepare a place for my people, if it were not so I would not have told you so. Look up for your redemption draws near, and have a productive day.

Confession

Heavenly Father, I humbly bow my heart to you today. Lord, where I have been guilty of practicing tradition in the past and even today? I am sorry Lord! Where I have persecuted your people with my tradition, please forgive me! Oh God break and destroy the seed and the root of every traditional mindset that are secretly imbedded in me. Your words declare that every root that my father has not planted shall be uprooted. Lord give me the grace to live by the power of your word and not by tradition in Jesus mighty name.

Day Fourteen

Raise Your Standard and Reap the Reward

Scripture: I Samuel 17:11 - 15

Many times we find ourselves in discomforting positions and situations with a mindset that we have already failed. Things look like they are not going to happen, but if we move away from that place we can reap great rewards. Raising the standard can mean that the things that have you bound, have to let you go because you shift position. When you move from that place of vulnerability you will reap great reward. David saw how much these men were afraid of the Philistine Goliath. If the Israelite soldiers had raised their standard they could have faced Goliath, but they could not because their mindset was at a crippling place. I want us to understand that as you raise your standard, you must have great expectation concerning quality and the result that you will get. Raising your standard as believers is very important, not just the church but the world at large. Whenever a man begins to raise his standard he shall reap from that place, because a level of boldness has overtaken him.

How does one raise his standard?

- ***One must be focused*** - You must be focused in that specific area of life that you need the standard to raise; but if you are fixated on what the enemy is doing then you cannot gain that confidence to raise your standard.
- ***You must believe in what you are doing*** - Believe in your move of changing your standard.
- ***Change your course of action.*** - You must be bold, ready and alert at all times and you will not be afraid to take on anything, and being ready for the next level, you will not panic and be broken down. If you understand the scriptures, you will find out that this goliath was the strong man, as his garment alone had some weight to it. For that type of garment to fit goliath it meant that goliath structure was heavy, strong. How could a little man fight this great giant?
- ***You have to face your fears*** - This means taking the first step to face head on the very thing that threatens you.

The bible declares that this goliath had the children of Israel at a place of bondage for so long, and he took pleasure in intimidating them. They could not fight him, they were afraid that he would defy them, speak cursed words at them and all this time they would stand down. They did not raise their standard simply because of fear. The bible speaks of the little boy David who was tending his father's sheep at the backside of the desert, and he was in obscurity. God is about to pull some people from the back side of the desert, as they are not cognizant of facts, or of present state. They have been prepared for such a time as this.

When I examined David's life, I have come to realize that David was anointed from a tender age, since God saw David as king. David saw himself however as a little shepherd boy, and so did his father who took care of the sheep. However, his brothers saw him as nothing beyond a shepherd boy.

- ***Accept who God has called you to be*** - Even when God has called you to be this great person the enemy may tell you otherwise and convince you, and the world at large may see you as insignificant, as nothing. The bible states that God demoted Saul, and Samuel the prophet was bawling and pining over Saul whom God had already rejected. God said, "I am sending you on an assignment; get up because I am sending you somewhere, to the house of Jesse. When you go there I will use you to anoint one of his sons because I call him to be king." So you must understand who God called you to be, not what is happening or what man is saying.

All of Jesse's sons who seemingly fit the part of king were present, but they were not anointed and the oil would not flow. The prophet asked Jesse, Is there were another son? He responded, yes there is a little one who watches over the sheep. I Samuel 16:11 KJV states, *"And Samuel said unto Jesse, Are here all thy children? And he said, there remaineth yet the youngest, and behold, he keepeth the sheep and Samuel said unto Jesse send and fetch him: for we will not sit down till he come thither."* At this point Samuel knew that God spoke yet the oil would not flow on the sons presented to him.

Samuel had a relationship with God and he knew that he did not make a mistake, and God cannot lie. The Father said yes, there is that little one (I Samuel 16:12). The Lord said, "Arise and anoint him for this is he." As David positioned himself to be anointed for the oil to be poured, there was a great task on David's life that he did not know about. There was a time coming for Goliath, the giant in the land to be slain.

Jesse sent David on an errand to take food to his brothers in the army and check on their wellbeing. David came at an opportune time and heard the Philistine giant defying the armies of the living God. His attention was brought to that place because he realized how rude Goliath was behaving, and as the giant stepped out the children of Israel would step back. The giant '*threw down the gauntlet*' to Israel and said, "Choose one of your men to fight me. If he wins and kills me, we will be your slaves; but if I win and kill him, you will be our slaves." That was the mistake he made! The giant saw the Israelites as insignificant, and David was furious at this mockery and asked, who is this uncircumcised philistine? Tell me what will happen to anyone who slay this giant? David saw himself as an accomplished warrior, a man who was skilled in warfare and slew both lion and beer and defended his sheep. Understand therefore that God was preparing David to fight one of his greatest battles ever.

There are times in your life when you are going through warfare and other issues, but some little mosquitos come to sing in your ears and suck your blood, and you use your hands and clap that thing.

Essentially, you don't know what God is preparing your hand to do, so in the end David was convinced that he was a warrior for Christ. He was in the backside of the wilderness and when the enemy animal came none of them could take out the sheep he slew them by using his bare hands. David did not see the children of Israel different from the sheep he had in the backside of the desert, and he saw the giant as a lion and a bear. You better see your problems as the thing you have been overcoming for years. In David's eyes the giant was just like one of those animals he used his bare hands to slay.

It is time to raise your standard and you will reap your reward. There are some high mountains that are way up above you, there are some people speaking some negative things over your life. The same way you killed the lion and the bear and take authority over the situations that face you in life is the same approach you should take for your present situation. Do not pay attention to the mouth that they use to curse you, just use your tried and proven weapon against the enemy who is the devil. Zechariah 4:6 KJV echoes, [6]*"Then he answered and spake unto me, saying. This is the word of the Lord unto Zerubbabel, saying, Not by might, nor by power, but by my spirit, saith the Lord of hosts."* God is saying that it is not by might or by power that your giant is going to come down, but it is by the spirit of the Living God.

Eliab saw David just as a shepherd boy who took care of his father's sheep similarly, Goliath saw him as a little boy, which can be viewed as an insult. However, The prophet saw David as a good little ruddy boy to look upon. Saul at one point saw David as his armor bearer. He called on David when he was distressed by an evil spirit, the bible tells us that David played the harp and warded off the evil spirit. Why do you think this same person who could ward off evil spirit can't take down Goliath? Although Jesse and others saw David as insignificant, God saw him as king. Who do you see yourself as today? David saw himself as a mighty warrior not only to fight lions but also bears.

David rose up in righteous indignation against the uncircumcised Philistine, but Eliab his brother accused him, Why did you come down here with your haughty spirit to make noise? David in self-defense asked, what have I done, Is there not a cause? Eliab and all David's brothers and the children of Israel could not face off with Goliath; but as soon as David raised the standard to take down the enemy, they had a problem with David as they did not realize that an enemy is an enemy. In I Samuel 17:32 KJV, David boldly declared, "... *Let no man's heart fail because of him; thy servant will go and fight with this Philistine.*" Do not allow your heart to fail; and maybe I am speaking to myself as well. Whatever is happening or whatever is coming up against you; it doesn't matter the weapons that they have, how they are big, mighty, their type of gun, witchcraft, etc. If God be for you then who can be against you; and if God speaks a word over your life as sure as night follows day, it shall come to pass.

Let me speak to the audience today! You may be worried about your stolen documents, what they are coming with next. God is saying to you this morning, do not allow your heart to fail you. Saul the king and the men of Israel made their complaint and they said, "See what this man is doing? He is defying Israel, he is rising up against us and we feel that we have no might of ourselves." The little ruddy boy saw their dilemma and assured them, "Let no man's heart fail him. Thy servant will go and fight with the Philistine." And although David said that, Saul said to David, "You are not able to go and fight with this Philistine because you are but a youth and he is a man of war from his youth."

Sometimes we see our battle based on historical facts but not understanding the effect of the powerful God we serve. There is a balm in Gilead, a mighty man of war, one who never sleeps or slumbers. God is getting ready to break on somebody's behalf. God is more than facts and the enemy is coming with facts. David said to Saul, "Listen, he may be a warrior from his youth but that is ok. He is not bigger than my God."

David presented his resume to Saul saying, thy servant kept my father's flock and when the lion and the bear came and took a lamb out of the flock, I went after him and smote him and delivered him out of his mouth. When he rose against me I caught him by his beard and smote him. You shall overcome! David took five smooth stones out of the river and the first one he fired connected Goliath, and he used Goliath's own sword and slew him. As you arise, position yourself and raise your standard, you shall reap your reward. So whatever situation, torment, fear you are going through and you feel all alone the God of your salvation will take care of you.

Confession

Oh my loving Father, I come before you one more time. I ask you oh Lord to search me and remove all careless and procrastinating habits from me and forgive all my sins. I ask you oh Father to give me the grace to raise the standards of my life. Please help me to be focused, believe in what I am doing and take authority over every intimidation and let me reap my rewards.

Day Fifteen

The Waters Will Recede

Scripture: Genesis 9:1 - 18; 7:15 - 24

God's covenant of promise still prevails against your deep waters. Waters can be seen as troubles, and the reverse is true. When you look at water being out of control, anything that it touches goes under. The word of God declares that when the enemy comes in like a flood the spirit of the Lord will lift up a standard against it, (Isaiah 59:19 KJV). For some of us there are troubles on our left and troubles on our right. We have been going through some deep waters, stress, some situations that you thought would subside. You thought something would happen now but every time you look it is another situation, sea coast, stream, river of water. 'Jordan' coming down on you with all kinds of trouble, causing you to be traumatized by the constant troubles. Some of us were strong, warriors, active, but we allow the bad news to take us to a place of faithlessness. We do not realize that all these things come to kill faith, and when your faith dies you no longer see God for who He is anymore.

I was driving over the weekend and my son did something very bad to me, and when I realize what he did I knew I was in a terrible state and needed deliverance. My son called me from a private number and disguised himself as calling from a particular police station, he asked, "Do you have a second child?" and called him by name. I said, "Yes." He continued, "We were doing some spot checks and we found him with a weapon." I was in the traffic and I said what weapon, gun? The only reason the gun came to my mind is the fact that I have been through a lot of trauma and hell; and so I live constantly on the edge.

My former pastor would often say that the anointing attracts trouble, and I can tell you that my life is full of trouble; and there are some days I feel like I can't go and can't pray. Job said, "Man that is born of a woman is of a few days and his life is filled with troubles," (Job 14:1 KJV). He also said, "*Though He slay me, yet will I trust in him: but I will maintain mine own ways before him*" (Job 14:15 KJV). When this prank officer spoke to me, I said, "Did you find him with a gun?" He said, "Mom, I can't disclose that information, but you need to come and report to us." Instantaneously, I felt a weakness coming up from my feet; and I did not feel an anointing to rebuke or speak in tongues (rabbahbahbahbah). I felt deep waters coming up on me, death coming up on my body. I wailed and said, "unoo a go kill me now, mi dead."

That was Friday, on Thursday during fasting service I was under a heavy anointing and now I feel death. I said, "Let me pull over. Sir, what now?" I heard the pickney laugh, I said "the blood of Jesus is against you and gave the phone to the passenger who was accompanying me." She said, "Rev. just turn off the air condition and pull down the window" as both of us were experiencing the same trauma. I concluded we need deliverance, we need help, something is wrong with us.

The tears were near, I was going to break and I tried consoling myself. I then said to myself, "Get a grip of yourself, you are in a bad state." When you have been constantly dealing with bad news it can't get any worse. It would be like the devil has a sledge hammer and keep hitting, but realize you are not breaking and he keeps hitting to say, "you are not coming down?" The intention is to shake you and for you to go down, as when one bad news comes it takes you into fear and distress. My son did not understand what he did to me, since you can't play those pranks with a person who has been in constant war.

I was told of a story of a soldier whose girlfriend playfully held his throat while he was sleeping and he felt threatened. He jumped up grabbed a knife and plunged it into her, thinking it was an attacker. A warrior does not play, as what you go through is real warfare. This devotion might not be for everybody but for those who go through real battles and distress. You are one whom the enemy is trying to kill, and every day that you get up you are fighting another war. I rebuked my son sternly, impressing upon him not to play those games with me because he knows what I go through.

I want to speak to some persons who are constantly going through battles as the Lord is saying the waters will not overtake you. He is giving a covenant of His promise to His beloved to say to you, whatever you are going through stand flat footed. He is God and He sees your tears, fears, agony and distress. He is making you His covenant of promise so that when the flood comes it will not kill you. It will not destroy you. When you see the rainbow remember his promise of assurance.

Men were on their way to a devil's hell! For 120 years Noah preached to a people that was stiff necked, when God gave Noah an instruction to build an ark because a day was coming, when he would take out the wickedness out of the land. God is enemy to the wicked and the wicked is an enemy to God; but the church cannot be an enemy to God, that is why we constantly get the word of warning to repent, and the word comes to cut. The word cannot be compromised, and for this reason we cannot minimize the gospel. We have to understand that the reason men are dying like this is because of the level of sin in the land. You have to allow the Lord to use you with His power and authority.

The waters of your life may threaten to drown you, the troubles heap up from bank to bank, bills to pay, school fees to pay, can't make two ends meet, sickness threatens, heart ache and headaches from ministry, warfare within and without. You may feel that your back is against the wall and you are screaming in fear and distress, hoping that the Lord will turn the tide around immediately; but the more you cry is the greater the trouble. Tell yourself this has an expiry date and it must end. You are going through your process, remain constant and faithful, God has not forgotten you, and know that the waters will recede.

A moment is coming when the land of problem is about to dry up on your behalf, and the fountains of the deep have to respond to God. God is about to remember you as you are going through. The enemy tried some things against your life, but do a prophetic declaration at this date and time. The water will not prevail against your life anymore or cover you anymore. There will be no dead situations in your life anymore, and you are about to live again; breathe, dance, sing, again. A stop order on your troubles is about to hit your life. Declare over your life, I am about to dance in this season! I am going to be laughing in this season! God is about to announce you.

There is an announcement about your victory and prosperity in the realms of the spirit. The spirit of excellence has established you because God remembers you. It is your season to dance, oh you are going to dance, it is your season to dance. Sound of victory, overcoming, loud testimony! Although your ship maybe rocking and your sails maybe torn, you will find shelter in the eye of the storm. You're Ararat, and your ship is about to rest upon the mount. Ararat means the curse is reversed. A 360 degree turn around! Reverse the stop order, stagnancy, troubles, pains. Access granted!

Your name is being called. High society is calling you, and may the favour of God find you. A reversing is here, so they can't stop you in this season. You are dancing in victory, and it is your hour to rise, shine. Shining season! The water is abating so see God moving for you, shifting some things. I see a cloud and it is coming! You are going! You are going! It is your season of healing, breakthrough, and overflow. My season has changed! It is your season to be anointed, to fasts and pray to go to your next level. The curse and the altar is reversed! No contrary wind and your wind of breakthrough and deliverance is here. You have no money in your pocket, can't keep a job, the marriage is bad, your change is here. Peace, joy, happiness.

They can't stop you! It's a run-away train. What is your name?

declare it in the atmosphere. Your season of afflictions die by fire! Mount Ararat is here to reverse every set-back. The ark rested! Take the rope off your neck prophetically. The devil wants lump in your breast, sickness in your womb, take it off. Every sickness that touch humanity shall stay far from you. You are anointed to cross over. You were wondering when is your season going to change. Your Ararat has come!

Some people who hate you are going to love you, and the favour of God shall find you. Point on your feet and declare that anywhere you walk you shall possess it. You are God's son and daughter. Favour shall locate you in this season. If you are studying, you shall be successful in your exams. The subjects are yours this year. Biopsy reports shall come up clean. Uncommon favour is your divine portion, Hallelujah. The anointing that is upon this devotional and it shall break every chain as you meditate on God's words today. You have cried long enough but your waters shall be abated. The waters have asswaged.

Confession

My heavenly Father, I come to you just as I am. Lord I ask that you purge and burn out of my heart every seed and root of fear and doubt. I stand in confidence in your Word that you will never leave me nor forsake me. Although the waters are raging on the outside I am safe in the ark of your presence. Therefore, Lord teach my heart not to fear the sound of the gushing waters, knowing that the waters will recede and your covenant of promise still stands.

Day Sixteen

God's Covenant of Promise Still Prevails Against Your Deep Waters

Scripture: Genesis 8:1 – 4; Genesis 9:13 – 17

The covenant of promise is described as a divine announcement of God's holy will to extend the benefits of God's unmerited grace.

There was an announcement made by God many years ago, that when you see the rainbow it is a promise that He will not destroy the earth with water again. We are reminded of this as over the last couple of days the heavy rains caused the waters to flow. Water can flow into some places and it looks terrible. God is still saying, "I am not going to destroy the earth with this anymore. When you see the rainbow just remember that it is still my covenant of promise." Now we benefit from his unmerited grace, in that, those who were willing to move by faith he received them, and they have now entered into a personal commitment with God. They bound themselves to him by ties of an absolute obligation. Noah was given no such requirement! This covenant was unilaterally granted by God. All of God's other covenants are mostly bilateral where the other party is required to simply respond. There was nothing that Noah could do after this that could have caused God to change his mind concerning His covenant of promise. The assurance of the rainbow was given whenever it rained heavily upon the earth, following the aftermath of the flood in Noah's time. God made the covenant unique as it was not just to Noah and his biological children and their descendants, but it was also to every creature on the earth. Even the most evil person can still benefit from this covenant of promise.

After the flood the bible declares that, "Noah built an altar unto God, and as he built it the fragrance that came from the altar came to the nostrils of God" (Genesis 8:21 KJV) At that time God repented of killing everybody on the earth with water, and that was the time God said He would no longer do that. This was the covenant of promise, the rainbow that Noah received that spans his descendants and is redound to us today. There will be tornadoes, volcanoes, tsunamis or mudslides but the promise of His covenant remains the same.

You may be encountering a deep storm, hurricane, flood or rain but the end has not come in destruction and flood and kill off the nation; and It is simply because of the covenant of the rainbow. Now, I want to put this in a spiritual way. When a man's ways please God, and he seeks and strives after His will to maintain a holy life; God is saying no matter what you are going through, here is my covenant of promise, and I will see you through. The bible says, if a man should come after him let him first deny himself, take up his cross, and follow him, (St. Luke 9:23 KJV).

The bible declares, "If we cannot be like a child we cannot serve him or enter the Kingdom of Heaven" (St. Matthew 18:3 – 4). A child is limited, dependent, not prideful or egotistic, they do not have the knowledge to do all of that as they are innocent. God is saying to His children, if you are not humble or have the personality of a child my kingdom is not for you. Jesus said, if anyone touch one of his little ones it is best for them to hang or drown themselves rather than touch his own (St. Matthew 18:6). When you serve God He is obligated to you to take care of you, because His word says it.

Some people behave like they serve God in vain and that is a myth. When you are serving God and you know that you are not deliberately committing sinful act you fear Him enough to do his will on a daily basis. God is obligated to you, so if His people are hungry or in pain God knows. If you are fearful and in distress He knows. You are not alone, your faith needs to take you to the place of the word and you need to maintain your position.

But the devil is so subtil as he takes us away from the word, the promise that braces us and cause for us to be contented in disobedience. He knows that if you are empowered he can't just walk up in your face; because he does not know what is going to happen next. You may just go into your (gun) barrel and bust a blood of Jesus and demons have to scatter (run away). He strategizes, he waits until you are weary. This is the word of God to you who are waiting in God. Why are you so perturbed? If you know that you are saved, Why are you in derision constantly?

The devil said to Jesus, "Ok, He will give his angels charge over you if you dash your foot against a stone," (Psalm 91:11). So the devil knows the word and he comes to contest God's people. But declare out loud to yourself even now, "Thy word have I hid in my heart that I will not sin against thee" (Psalm 119:11). "Thy word is a lamp unto my feet, and a light unto my path" (Psalm 119:105). Teach me oh Lord to wait upon you, because your word says, "They that wait upon the Lord shall be as mount Zion and they shall not be moved" (Pslam 125:1). They that wait upon the Lord God, He shall renew their strength. They shall run and not be weary, walk and not faint. "They shall mount up with wings as eagles, (Isaiah 40:31).

Are you crazy enough to wait upon God? Sometimes you are waiting on God and man consider you to be crazy. You are moving in faith and you said I am not touching it (sin), and they say you are mad. But some people need to step away from the toxic environment, ways and behaviour. We need to draw in a corner, take up our bibles and give the devil a war, we are not alone "*But the Lord is with me as a mighty terrible one: therefore, my persecutors shall stumble, and they shall not prevail: they shall be greatly ashamed; for they shall not prosper: their everlasting confusion shall never be forgotten*" (Jeremiah 20:11).

I want to root you up from where you are, so that your faith will rise up to the place of promise. Oh that your faith will rise up to the covenant of promise. Some of you do not know who you are, how effective you are under Holy Ghost order. You are suffering for far too long, so you better open up your mouth and command a thing and watch it come to pass. In the name of Jesus! When demons come to your home you have power in your belly to plead the blood and they have to take away themselves. You do not have to walk and look over your shoulders. People throw powder on your place, declare that the Lord has given me power and authority. Whatsoever I bind on earth is bound in heaven and whatsoever I loose on earth is loosed in heaven, (St. Matthew 18:18 KJV).

During this week I got a call that thieves broke into my restaurant and stole some stuff, cases of meats etc, and the chef went to the police station to lodge a complaint. They asked for the owner to come instead, but I didn't go because I was scheduled to preach the gospel. So I told the staff to clean up the place and cook, but I went to the altar and cried out to the Lord. A wanted man cannot show up himself, he will be locked up. I cried out, "God I can't go, it is because of you why I am hated, so you take care of my business." When you know who you are stay steady in the presence of God. You go on your knees and pray, Lord locate all of those thieves, your stomach shall be sick, there shall be trouble with your body. You must confess and come and pay back what you stole.

I recall a story I heard, that a man stole some electrical wires and the owner went to the obeah man (wizard who works witchcraft) and the thieves had to return the wires at the man's gate. If heathen can do that what about me who serve the true and living God; the big bad warrior in God? When I fast and pray and leave it in God's hands I do not want outside help to defend me, because the protector works on my behalf. Because I am declaring Jesus I am now an arch enemy, but I am a beneficiary of the covenant of promise according to my God.

So who are you in Zion? Who are you? You are a citizen, an ambassador. When some people see you they have to sniff the blood (of Jesus), and some who are demonized the demons will scream out in them. Recently I was in Stony Hill and a young lady seem to be of unsound mind, from a far she started declaring, "I am not talking to you today." I realize that the demons were stirred up in her, because of the radiance that was coming from me, and it began to put her in trouble. I am speaking to the warriors, the overcomers, those who carry the DNA of Jesus. I can't touch anything unless God says touch it. If he does not say touch it leave it alone, as God says he will fight the battle.

A lot of you should have died but the gun was stuck permanently. They can't harm you because you are covered. 'Hi five' someone and tell them that the gun got stuck. "*Blessed is the man that walketh not in the counsel of the ungodly, nor standeth in the way of sinners, nor sitteth in the seat of the scornful. 2 But his delight is in the law of the Lord; and in his law doth he meditate day and night*" (Psalm 1:1 - 2 KJV). They can't touch you, the harder they come, the harder they will fall because there is a covenant of promise. Shout it out loud, there is a covenant of promise. Some of you have some court cases, let the Lord fight the battle for you.

I had an insurance policy and I was diligently paying, and my husband asked, "Why are you giving this lady your money every day? Concerning my husband, If I do not discern that something is off he does. Now each time I am to pay the policy my husband is upset, and he said "I do not trust this lady; she is eating your money." I retorted, "nothing like that I am issued a receipt for each payment." One day the agent informed me that she is migrating and I should continue making payments to the bank. I paid once and it was accepted, and the subsequent payment could not be uploaded to the insurance company system. Essentially, the lady absconded with my money.

Some people are in serious problems with me, so I said God I do not want to pray one or a piece of prayer for this person. I fought until I was refunded one of the policies, but the others were not refunded. When the inside agent from the insurance company began explaining all the benefits of my policies after five years I was in awe. I did not understand the benefits that came with my policies. This dishonest agent was so smart, she set up the insurance into companies so that the payments were made annually and it would not have lapsed; because there was an incubated period before that happens. Can you imagine deceived for five years and being ignorant of my benefits?

I am not dunce neither is it difficult for me to understand, but I had to ask the person to explain to me again, what are the benefits that accompany my policies? She said after 10 years I would receive a moratorium (cessation of payment). Now I realize that I lost five years of benefits. I am saying this to say that, the coverage that God gives us as Christians, a lot of us are not cognizant of our benefits. We do not understand what we can get under this comprehensive blood coverage. It is more than all the insurance companies that give good benefits and interest rates.

The blood coverage that comes from heaven says that I am anointed and appointed to walk into some dead situations and they come back to life. Who's going to buy oil and powder when you should have the blood? What are you doing with machete and carnal weapons, arguing with people? All you have to do is go on your face, as it may be long but not forever. If you trust in God's amazing grace He will see you through. Touch your neighbour and say it is time for us to pull from this insurance company.

Some of us are in Zion a long time and allowing some people to come and steal our benefits, the same way this dishonest woman stole my benefits of five years. This is how some of us are not aware that when you come under the blood, people just can't touch you. When you are under the blood, God gives security and hears every evil conversation. He hears what people are maliciously saying about you, just as He heard when the gunman said this bullet is for you, but you declare your blood will not be shed. When you overheard them calling your name, you know that the anointing on your life cause you to carry a heavy weight in the realms of the spirit.

There was another personal incident where my son was driving the bus, and during a police spot check the insurance expired that day. When the documents were checked and it was discovered that I am the owner, the officer retorted, "Oh is the feisty woman bus." I am a decent woman but because of the blood of Jesus I am a target. When you stand up for God satan knows you good, but they can't touch you because the covenant of promise works for you. You can sleep in your bed undisturbed. No rat bats, or satan descendants can approach because you are anointed and appointed.

God is saying, it does not matter what you are going through he will always remember you. Say Lord remember me: in my deep distress, when I can't find food to eat, send the children to school, when pain is rocking my body. Oh Lord, Remember me! You do not understand that when God gives coverage, He covers you well. When He said you are blessed curse cannot style you... a secular song says it best, "a wha du dem, a wha du dem dem dem, an mi nuh know oh.." but catch the rhythm of this song:

"Under the blood, mi under the blood, rise up God

Pickni yu under the blood, mommy and daddy,

under the blood, my business under the blood,

my job under the blood, under the blood,

I, wi, I wi, I, wi under the blood…pull up!"

The bible states that the waters covered the face of the earth, and every living thing, breathing the breath of God was dead, saving for the eight that entered the ark. When God covers you, you are comprehensively covered. When God promises you something, sit down on the rhythm and ride. He is not a God to make mistake, or to lie. Some of you need to go back in the barrel and say God, I pull up the chronicles. I remember when in your word you said this about my life… The bible relates that the king could not sleep. Mordecai did something good but it was forgotten for a while, as the king had insomnia, and he began reading the chronicles and came across the record of this man's good deed of saving his life. He said, "hold on, what was done for this man who saved my life?" They responded, nothing. He called one of his servants, Haman and said "what should be done for this man who saved my life?" He said "get a big horse, place him on it, give him your ring, take him through the town and allow everyone to honour him." He thought it would have been him. The king listened and drop the bombshell, it would be Mordecai, (Esther 6).

There are some Mordecais, whom God says He is going to restore their barns, he is going to recall the chronicles. Some people whom you helped, like the church yard that you swept for fourteen (14) years, God says, "I am pulling out the chronicles." God does not work anybody and do not pay them. Some people do not understand how much they are missing out when a work day is called at church and they refuse to show up. It is clear that you do not know the bible, you are ignorant of the intricacies of his promises. When you work for God he honours and blesses not only you but your generation. If the king could have saved Mordecai for saving his life, what about you who feed homeless people, send children to school etc. sow into the life of a needy person who has no dinner.

The bible said, I was thirsty and you gave me water to drink, I was hungry and you fed me, I was in prison and you visited me. But you say when? How come? He said the least that you have done unto these little ones you have done it unto me (St. Matthew 25:35 – 40). We are flesh and blood and it will rot, but our soul shall make it into heaven. Know that whatever you do for God he will reward you. Genes 8:1, "*And God remembered Noah, and every living thing, and all the cattle that was with him in the ark: and God made a wind to pass over the earth, and the waters asswaged*"

God remembered Noah and nature responded. God remembered Noah and the fountains of the deep stopped, the windows of heaven were stopped. When He remembered Noah, the rain from heaven restrained, and the water returned from off the earth continually. The waters abated because God remembered Noah. When God remember you, things will happen, and God put a calm to the situation. Say, Lord put a calm to my condition. What are you going through? What is the situation that your life is under? What is the enemy trying to do to you? God is about to remember you, and God's covenant of promise still prevails and the deep waters cannot drown you.

Confession

Holy Father, righteous and true. Broken and contrite I come before your throne, needing your grace and mercy in every area of my life. Lord I confess all my sins of omission and commission, every filthiness of the spirit and of the flesh. I ask you Lord to rid me of all impatience when my waiting on you becomes a weight, in Jesus Christ mighty name, amen.

Day Seventeen

Behold, Look! I am Doing a New Thing

Scripture: Isaiah 43:1 - 5: 18 - 19

God is saying to his people, behold I am doing a new thing, look out for it. If God is doing a new thing, and we are not looking out for it, so we can literally miss what God is doing. The word of God to you this morning is, "Forget the former things and watch what I will do." Trials are inevitable, as the scripture says when you go through the waters, not if. He said he will be with you in all things and all times; so you need to understand that there are times you will go through things, and it does not mean that God has abandoned you.

Trials are inevitable and we are not exempt from the affairs of this life, but we need to understand that as we go through the mire and clays of life we serve a God who neither sleeps or slumbers. Isaiah spoke to God's people. The children of Israel were captives in Babylon, the 70year period of exile where they were held against their will. They were scarred and in deep depression, they were desperate and their circumstance of captivity caused them to be bound and shackled.

When discouragement comes and the fires of hell and life hits, if you do not know who you serve you will get discouraged; and you will feel like God has somehow forgotten you. The songwriter penned it and said "I have proven times and times again that God is able to take care of His people." Today I want to tell you that if you are living by the laws and precepts of God He is obligated to take care of you because of His word. He says heaven and earth shall pass away but my word shall never pass away.

He says he is going to shelter you in the storm as his children/disciples. Yes, you will go through the fire and the water, but it will not totally wipe you out, since there is a rhema that is over your life. Isaiah told the people to be encouraged, be strong. God says look not at the things that you have gone through, forget the past concerning the things you have been through. God is saying forget it because it will not dictate to your future. Do not be stuck in the past because God is saying behold I am doing a new thing. Do not be seduced by the enemies because God says, I am doing a new thing.

Look out! There is a release! So many of you have gone through trauma and it brought so much fears on you. It is like you are crippled, and a level of impotency has come upon you and you do not know how to fight. The enemy has brought you to a place where you feel fear, rejection, no help for you. I am here to tell you that there is a balm in Gilead, and it does not matter how you have been opposed, or what men are saying about you. God is saying I foreknew you before you knew yourself.

I am the Lord who has formed you oh Jacob, be not afraid oh Israel for I have formed thee, I have called you by name thou art mine. If you look at a brand such as WATA or a product manufactured by GRACE they belong to their manufacturer, and so God is saying those who belong to me, I have labelled and fashioned them. I have called them by my name, they belong to me. Will God have you to die, or leave you in a place of torment for the rest of your life? Man may say this is it for you, but God is not like the unjust judge. You may go through some storms in your life, but God is saying it will not kill you.

Those storms of life that have caused you to be depressed and put a rope around your neck, God is saying, "Look, I am doing a new thing. I am changing that; I have been giving you the ammunition to overcome for so long, but you can't even see it because of the trauma." Doubt, fear, faithlessness. God is saying, "Get on board and get in position; that which is so hard God says he is bringing it down to a level playing field." Yes! The warfare is intense. The enemy says go and take up some liquor, get a shot of rum and boom and hold a meds with the people in the world. That is not working out for you, as that is a lie from the pit of hell, and God is not a man that he should lie.

Isaiah 43:3 emphatically proclaimed, "*For I am the Lord thy God, the Holy One of Israel, thy Saviour: I gave Egypt for thy ransom, Ethiopia and Seba for thee." God is saying you are precious and honourable and I will give men and people for thee. Fear not for I am with thee.*" If God is saying the bull is raging but fear not, it means that the cow can't buck you to kill you. You shall not die! His word is a protection it forms a shield for you. Psalm 3:1, "*O Lord you are a shield for me, the glory and the lifter up of my head.*"

When you come into the things of God you are sheltered and covered; you have a covenant with God. I had a discussion in recent times where someone was relating about the 'guard rings' which is witchcraft protection, and they saw how it worked. The Holy Spirit dropped it in my spirit that this is no guard, but an evil covenant that the person has entered in. When you are guarded by somebody you are sheltered, but with a guard ring, you have to make an evil covenant with an evil person. Essentially the wizzard released a demon upon the person which is stronger than the one that is oppressing him. Therefore, whatever he used seemed to be working, but it is a hoax, and only results in more problems for the individual who is seemingly being guarded.

God wants to give you a protection that is second to none, that is enshrined in His promises. When you hinge your faith on the Word of God, it empowers your spirit man and take you to a place of super-expectation. The Centurion said to Jesus, "Just speak the word and I believe that my servant is healed. I am a man of authority and when I speak it is unquestionable." Jesus exclaimed "wow! I have not seen such great faith in Israel." Where is your faith today? Do you have the faith to believe for the newness you have been hoping for with abated breath? God is doing it in this season, and it may not look or feel like anything that you have ever encountered. Forget about your past pain and embrace your present and future victory. Newness is pronounced upon you today, receive it in Jesus Mighty name.

Confession

Dear heavenly Father, I thank you for the invitation to come boldly to your throne, where I will obtain mercy, and find grace in time of need. As I come oh God, I repent before you for the many times my eyes were blinded to what you were doing; because I was focused on the problem and not on you. Lord I humbly ask for your forgiveness and open the doors and windows of my heart to see the new thing that you are doing with me in this season, amen.

Day Eighteen

Prophetic Acceleration

Scripture: Amos 9:13 – 15

When we hear of acceleration our minds conceive speed, and instantaneously things can move from one place to another. I can be in a dung hill this moment and another moment I am on my mountain top. Somebody may ask, how did you get there? One thing I know about God is that '*favour aint fair*,' and when God is about to rise up a man He will take him out of his down, desolate place. Even when man says you are not qualified, his opinion has nothing to do with the move of Almighty God in the situation.

As we stand in position for acceleration, we need to understand that we must be positioned for this great move. The bible declares in Amos 9:1 KJV, "*I saw the Lord standing upon the altar: and he said, Smite the lintel of the door, that the posts may shake: and cut them in the head, all of them; and I will slay the last of them with the sword: he that fleeth of them shall not flee away, and he that escapeth of them shall not be delivered.*" Whenever God wants to do something in our lives He has to take us into a dung hill position, to allow our feet to slip from under the carpet. There are times we are standing in a mis-aligned position that is not God's will and so He allows the painful situations to bring transformation in our lives, God will permit the enemy to invade and destroy as seen in scriptures.

Amos had a vision of the Lord standing by the altar, and he saw the Lord at the right hand of the temple, supervising the work of judgment concerning Israel, because Israel was in a backslidden state. Now God was standing and He poured out His judgment, but even in judgment God knows how much to allow upon us for His name to be glorified. One of the instructions that God issued to the angel was to strike the door post so that it would shake. It is widely believed that structurally the door post is the strongest part of the house, and so if the door post is broken the whole house may cave in.

There are times you hear some earthquakes in the realms of the spirit, and it is a shaking of things in order. God was shaking back the children of Israel into alignment by allowing destruction to come upon them. Why? Because of sin. Whenever man goes into apostasy, watch the hands of God dealing with them. The bible declares, there was a shaking and they could not escape, even if they climbed to a high mountain, dig a hole in hell, God will be there. They could not escape the judgment of God. The bible says, "I will set my hand of iron upon them and not of wood." God permitted some things to happen. Even the covenant of promise and blessings outlined in Deuteronomy 28:1 – 14 was shifted from them.

God is a covenant keeping God, and if we are not aligned to the precepts and principles of God, then his hands are going to cause a shifting. When man becomes disobedient God will allow him to feed from it and reap the consequence. Understand that we will not see the goodness of Almighty God until we get back in alignment. Like Israel, were now in a position to be shifted into humiliation. An illustration was done in church where sand was poured into a sift and at the end the rubble, stones, and waste was thrown away and the refine product remained, and it would be used to build the house. I want to declare to you that God is doing some sifting for a refinery product, and as we align ourselves to God, then we shall have some loud testimonies. He is looking for faithfulness in this season. One thing you should know about God is he cannot bless muck. It does not matter how you pray and fast. If you are in muck God will not bless you; and although favour is not fair, your life of sanctification speaks for you.

Have you ever seen a farmer planting seeds? There are some bad crops that he has to discard, some grapes that he finds worms in and he may have to throw them away; and the best ones will be secured and placed in the ground for them to grow. These are the things that are happening in Zion. a modern Jesus and a modernized church; but God is the same God yesterday today and forever. I do not know when or how, but if you maintain your position He will do it for you.

You may have struggled, been in derision for years but there is a speed that is accompanying you. There is an acceleration! God says He is going to do it for you, He is going to move somebody from zero to a hundred, and hell cannot stop it. Jesus Christ of Nazareth! I hear restoration is coming. Declare out loud, Lord restore my barns. The locusts, palmer worms, canker worm have eaten up some crops and things, but the Lord thy God in His love and mercy shall restore. I declare restoration in the name of Jesus Christ! I believe this is called prophetic acceleration. When you begin to prophesy some things, some people are going to think that you are mad, but when they see the production they will know that nothing about you is ordinary.

Speak to a neighbour and a friend, for if you get caught up in the spirit, you will not be ordinary, and people in the natural realm will think you are losing your mind. Things must be different, you will walk and talk, and preach different. Breakthrough, healing and deliverance will not come with you merely sitting down, so you have to position yourself, hallelujah. When man starts to pray demons start to tremble, and every stronghold must break away. Every high thing must come down. Appreciate that It is not by might or by power but by the spirit of the living God.

Education and theology cannot bring breakthrough and deliverance, but when you fast and pray and position yourself, and refuse to compromise, you will get breakthroughs. You will speak a word and watch it come to pass. Whatsoever you bind on earth is bound in heaven and whatsoever you loose on earth is loosed in heaven, (St. Matthew 18:18). The just man shall live by faith. You must move into a prophetic faith in this season, you are crossing over into it. Something has to break, it has to break!

When we speak about acceleration, we speak of the speed of God; now you see me and now you don't. It is the mystery of God, and it is going to move on some people's behalf. It will turn your water into wine, and turn your mess into a message. It is the time to get crazy. A secular artiste sang 'the people a mad out,' however, he does not understand what he is saying. Mad out is when a Christian turns his pot down and die of hunger for Jesus (fast), consequently punishing your flesh. You put down the nice delicious food and decide to fast and pray, for something has to break, limitations, set-backs must break. The word of God declares that these things do not come except by fasting and prayer, (St. Matthew 17:21 KJV).

I hear a victor's call and I shall overcome. When acceleration steps in, it means whatever is out of alignment, shall return to order. A lot of us have some pains in our bodies and if they come back tomorrow we have to take the medication. Some have sleepless nights, others believe for the healing of the flu, but not the cancer. Many of us should have been some millionaires, but because we are out of alignment we cannot even find bus fare. When you take your vehicle for alignment and it is placed on the stand, it is tested in several ways: a crab walk (a four-wheel steering setting), and the steering mechanism cannot control the vehicle.

Some things are out of control but God is saying I remember my people. In Amos 9:13 - 15, God declares that he remembers his people, the same way he remembered Noah. What is your name? release it in the atmosphere and declare that God remembers (your name). He remembers your children, your marriage, God remembers His promise. Every prophetic word that was released upon your life from the mouth of a true prophet; whatever you have not walked into as yet I release it upon your life. There is a set time for God to move on your behalf. For Noah, it was not that He was not in God's thoughts or mind, but there was a set time for God to move on his behalf. God has a set time of tomorrow to move for us, but we get weary today and quit today. But Acceleration is on it's way, a sudden shift from nothing to something, from fear to instant faith, there is a speed that is announced on your behalf in the realms of the spirit.

Confession

Oh Most Holy Father, here I am one more time before you. Lord I ask that you forgive me for every limitation I have placed on you with my limited understanding. May you remind me Holy Spirit that when man promotes he may be inclined to look at my past; but when you are ready to promote you take me from where I am to where I need to be in an instant.

Day Nineteen

Double For Your Trouble

Scripture: Job 42:10

We are in the season of loud testimonies. Crazy things shall happen, must happen, and will happen, something has to break. This is the season of completion, for your friend, and family. It is time to release control and trust the divine; for anything forced under this energy or touches this speed backfires. You are being asked to step into the flow. What the enemy meant for bad God has turned it around for your good. The enemy thought that he could have mis-used and abused Job, for though satan buffeted Job, it was meant for bad but God has turned it around for his good.

A lot of us are saying, God what is going on? The enemy has been trying some fast ones. But we need to focus on verse 10 of the text, "*And the LORD turned the captivity of Job, when he prayed for his friends; also the LORD gave Job twice as much as he had before.*" (Job 42:10 KJV). Now you are seeing the product of Job's process. Whenever you see recovery it precedes a downhill. When you see double fold it means some great things were lost before. Double doesn't just hit anybody like that. You would have gone through some valleys, reached rock bottom, gone through some deep weather, then comes the double. God says I am come to deliver, set free, break the yokes and lift every burden off you. It does not matter how much you have cried in the past; your double is coming.

There was this man in the land of Uz and his name was Job, and he was described as upright, faithful to God and an example of righteousness; he was different. The bible declares there was no man like Job in the entire earth, since he walked upright with God and the blessings of God was upon him because he acknowledged God. God placed the character of Job in the presence of his enemy. He went to sacrifice peradventure his children sinned in their heart, as he believed in holiness and righteousness. God boasted on Job, but can God boast about you? The wicked devil presented an argument to God about Job, he said, "How can he not be faithful when you put an edge around him, blessed him, and all is well?" God said to Satan, "You do not understand this boy. He praised me whether or not things are well or food is on his table." God was confident that this boy would serve him.

What befell Job was as a result of God's communication with Satan, and Job was not knowledgeable of what was happening. It was something that God and the devil was speaking about; a point of contention between God and Satan and had nothing to do with Job. I had a conversation with my son who recently had a miracle child, who is now 6 months old (at the time of writing) and she had to be resuscitated 5 times. I said to him "look at this child, nothing about her is ordinary." Let me tell you about purpose. Purpose can never be ordinary. You are going to see some pain, warfare in your purpose. It comes with a lot of agony.

At the time of Jesus' birth, there was no room for Him in the inn, and everybody was born in the hospital but no room for him. He was among the horses and goats. How can He be God and there was no room for him in the hospital? There is something about the people who are special and unique, your warfare is also unique and detrimental. The spirit of death is always after purpose, so when you see purpose it is a battlefield. 'You lick me down a drop a ground, I am going to bounce right back, I am a hard man to die.' My purpose can't die, it has to live, overcome, and produce loud testimony. Your testimony can't be ordinary and regular, sounding like everybody's. It cannot be, once I was blind but now I can see. It must be something different. It has to be a dead and wake condition. Gun man tried to kill you but you are still here. The rapist came but you are still here. Abused rejected but still here. Declare, I am still here! The reason you are still here is because of purpose.

Saul said, "Let me give David my daughter so that I can kill him." The enemy will give you his best to kill you. Some of you, your name is dead and wake, but you still have a sound and a speed, still here. They made your casket but up until now you can't lay down in it. You are too big for it. Your blood is boiling, you can't cool. Nothing on you is cold, life! Life! Life! If God is giving you double for your trouble it means you are Cinderella, but don't think about cuteness now, Cinderella was the step-daughter. The other two princesses did nothing, if God is going to give Cinderella the king, it must mean that she is special.

Some people do not understand how special you are. They are fighting you but they are fighting happiness, the anointing. Lucifer had something in his belly like a pipe, just like you have a sound in your belly. When you release this sound Obeah, gun, backfire. God says. "I will prepare a table before thee in the presence of your enemy," (Psalm 23:5).

When the discussion occurred between Job and God, Job's friends thought that based on the results and what matriculated, Job had sinned. Warn your detractors that they should not trouble you in this season. I am coming up on the rough side of the mountain. Leave me alone because destiny is calling me to another level. They will hold conferences, have round table talks over your name, but they do not understand you have a good character. The conversation they are having is ashes to ashes and dust to dust. Because you are so special, those who are having conversations about you, means it has surpassed the natural and has reached into the realms of the spirit. It becomes a spiritual conversation. Nothing earthly can be done about it.

The warfare is intensified, but it is for a greater glory. New levels, signs and wonders, for the deaf to hear, dumb to see, the leprous to be cleansed. Go into the bar and declare life and watch a dead man get up and shout a hallelujah. Some of you miss it because you live in the realms of the physical you can't hear anything spiritual. You are not feeling, hearing, seeing, tasting, smelling spiritually everything is physical. Some people have not passed that level. In some seasons you have to get rid of some friends, companions. You are going through hell and you can't carry some people with you, it is not my permanent address. No present situation is forever, and some people have written you off because they think that your present situation is permanent. They better be your friend now because tomorrow this time is double-double. Tomorrow when the seasons, address, and grace change, you will not be looking for friends.

Pardon me but God uses me differently. Have you ever heard about bedroom bully? Some people are anointed bully that they want to ride on your back like cow, but let me go. They want to be identified with you, not when you were in the valley, but when you come out of the valley. Some people who should have been there with you when you are going through deep waters forsake you. Job said, "It was my own acquaintances, those whom I went to the house of God with. When they were in trouble, I sat in sack cloth and ashes." Sometimes God has to remove the rug from under your feet to get rid of some vampires.

The bible said, when Job lost everything the only family member he had left was his wife, and at that time his wife was like a thorn in his flesh. In my opinion she said, "What kind of asset are you now, curse God and die." Some people will be with you as long as you are up and running. Some will be friends as long as you look nice. The moment you can't do what they asked you to do, they say the leverage has changed. Job's three friends came and accused Job of being in sin. They should have been in a position to say, this is not you? Now the character that Job had was a righteous one, of sound character, he was exemplary. These friends should have known that.

You can trust people whether or not they are saved, so when somebody fears God you trust that they would not do certain things. You can speak about their character and the things they have heard over a period of time. When some of us hear some rumors about people, we join Satan and mud up the person's name and dig up some things before the person got saved. His friends said, "Guess what, you sinned against God so do something about yourself." His wife questioned him with disgust, "Are you going to keep your integrity? Curse God and die." They think you are done but you are just coming. They don't know you are building to be blessed. I feel the Holy Ghost!

Sometimes you are going through some situations, you have to say keep me through Lord Jesus keep me through, there is a race I must run so keep me Jesus. Keep me through Jesus every second, minute, hour. I am crawling, creeping, rolling but I am coming. The battle may be hot and the conflict sore, it is rough but keep pressing, pressing, press, press, press. Don't backslide, don't back-down. We reverse every order that stand against your life, Run! Run the race. You may not understand what is going on, you feel death coming, but you are still maintaining your praise. There is a road upon your praise but you can't afford to miss it. It is the roughest season, it is rough and tough and you have gone through a Job situation, you lost some crops, season, but restoration. Band your belly and bawl. Give God a praise!

In verse six of the text, Job lamented, "*Wherefore I abhor myself and repent in dust and ashes.*" (Job 42:6 KJV). Sometimes you are wondering, what did I do? You search yourself but can find no answer. Have you ever been there? You are wondering, what sins did you commit, when, where were you disobedient to God? What caused this calamity and trauma? Some of us know what it is to be traumatized, and have your faith killed. When my last son was a baby he would say, "Mommy I am 'trampletize.' The devil is trying to trample your home and make you feel hopeless.

When everything was taken from Job, God went back to Satan and boasted while Job was still wailing. Job said, "What is this? My children are dead." He lost his taste bud, he felt his hair standing on his hand, thinking a duppy was passing. Maybe Job was binding witchcraft but there was none, but the Lord was crushing Job for a new level. Sometimes you see some pretty people come before you and the Holy Ghost turn them over with some trials because they are so pretty. God says, "Let me give you more grace and anointing, take this trial." And when you think it is over, he sends some persecution." Your tongue is too pure, but some tongues rise up against you for you to curse, but you cry, God what is this? God says, "Now I will give you the prophetic and your tongue shall roll." Your hands are pure and God says, "Take this healing grace." Not every warfare is from Satan. God is stretching you for you to birth out and a different sound to come out of you.

I saw a young lady who was so small in body, but her pregnancy expanded all parts of her body. Some of the times when we are going through we are swollen from the trials. Job received double because he was good. Some of the time you are saying God, "Where are you?" It is because you are special, you are not cursed, so the warfare and rejection you go through is because God is marking you. Give God a praise and A worship right here.

"Wherefore I abhor myself and repent in the dust and ashes." (Job 42:6 KJV). Job despised himself. Have you ever been there where the devil flogged you and you say, "I am tired of this, the struggles, the rejection?" Job was a man that God loved, but his agony distorted his voice, not even his servants knew his voice anymore. When he called on his servants he lost the power that he once had. Job said, "If I have sinned let a next man see my wife's nakedness." It was a shame for another man to look upon your wife's nakedness. What have I done? Why am I suffering so much? Whom have I offended? Have you ever gotten to the place where you hate yourself?

I don't know what I am living for, might as well everything fail; baby it is purpose. Job was at a place where he despised himself and felt rejected. Everybody talked about him. I can imagine they were saying, "what a piece of curse. You don't hear what is happening to Job? Him look mash up, skin dirty, and smell stenchy." Job had to be out in the yard filled with sores, which are raw, broken and painful places on the body. Those who came did not have an encouraging word.

All the people that you thought would have supported you, laughed at your calamity. But hold on my child, your joy comes in the morning. All that you are going through, there is a double that is coming for your trouble. No Christian carrying an anointing is exempted from going through hell. The community will call you obeah worker, but woe be unto the man that call evil good and good evil. They ran and spake all manner of evil against you, but God deserves a praise right here.

Job despised himself, and now he came to a place where he was now repenting. He began to reminisce on in his pain and all that he had gone through. He cursed and repented the very day he was born, he said, "Cursed be the day that a man son was born, cursed be the day of conception." When the sun rose up and there was an announcement made, he cursed everything but he did not curse God. Maintain your position, and stay at the altar because the enemy wants to dry up your prayer life in warfare. Job began to reflect on himself and he repented of his complaint against challenging God. He repented about his despair, statement of darkening wisdom by word without knowledge.

A time is coming, when you shall be restored, as the Lord is going to contend with your contenders. The Lord is about to give you double for all of your trouble. Double-double! Double-double! Double-double! The Lord restored Job in a double way, and the Lord turned the captivity of Job when he prayed for his friends. The Lord gave him twice as much as he had before.

Acceleration in this season, and God is about to move in a way where some people are going to say how come. He is going to turn your weeping into dancing. In Job 42:11 KJV. All his relatives came and ate bread with him, and gave him comfort. The Lord has brought up on him. Everyone gave him an earring of gold." When Job was in captivity there was none to comfort him, but as soon as things changed everyone showed up.

Some people are going to come in your season of victory with an ulterior motive, so reject their gift. Some people are anointed bully, that is, if you do not pray and they do not get a prophesy they do not come around you again. It is about to get warm. When you see some people coming to connect do not connect with them. The double-double is about to hit you. The speed, acceleration is about to hit you.

Job was blessed and when God restored he could not count his blessings. When man does it they talk about what they did, but when God restores, he places you where you should have been in the first place. When God restores a barn no man can take glory for what the

Lord has restored upon him, Hallelujah! You, yes you, in this season the Lord is about to grant you good success. In this season no wicked man shall oppress you. Neighbour, the sun shall not smite you by day nor the moon by night. Neighbour! Neighbour! Get ready to build, dance, smile. Sing! Your time of weeping is over, there is something different, loud testimonies.

There is a shaking going on in the camp of your enemy; oppressor, shake them out. Give God a mighty Praise! Double grace, double favour, double in your ministry, no weapon risen up against you shall prosper; but scatter by fire. In the latter days of Job's life, what he did not receive when he was young he got it in the latter season. This instruction is for you, place your hand on your belly, shout a mighty hallelujah. Let there be restoration right now. Everything that has been sabotaging your life, I declare victory with speed, acceleration, in the name of Jesus. You are coming out of every frustration that was against your life, right now!

Confession

Oh Lord I come to you this day asking for your forgiveness and pardon. Oh God wash me and purify my heart from every known and unknown sins. During the times when I hit rock bottom and went through deep waters, there were days when my thoughts strayed from your presence please forgive me LORD, in Jesus name.

Day Twenty

Even Nature Responds to Jesus: (What Measure of Faith Do You have?)

Scripture: St. Matthew 14:23 - 36

If nature itself responds to Jesus, then we are confident enough to stand still and see His operation even in the most boisterous wind. The disciples went off to go over on the other side, while Jesus went to pray. After prayer Jesus saw the need to go where the disciples were and to be with them. Before Jesus appeared the bible declared they were in the middle of the sea and there was a storm that hit them. The wind began to blow boisterously; and some versions say the wind was contrary. The disciples sought a way to row themselves to safety, but it was to no avail. At this time, it was approximately 3 A.M to 6 A.M, as described by St. Mark 6:47 - 49 KJV; accordingly, it suggested that the boat was in the middle of the sea. By this time, they were already exhausted by the sea roaring against the waves and the heaviness of the wind. The bible said, "The storm was great" (St. Mark 4:37 KJV).

If we should roll back the curtains, there were many acts of miracles that had already taken place in the eyes of the disciples. They just encountered Jesus using two fishes and five loaves to serve an entire multitude. They were in the atmosphere of signs and wonders because they were walking with Jesus. Trouble hit them and they began to walk and wail; but as you walk on this Christian journey you do not know what you will encounter.

Does your faith operate in the place where there seems to be no hope? The disciples were distressed because of the boisterous winds. Some of us are prayer warriors and over-comers but when the wind hit us, we forget that we are over-comers. Every warfare is not the same but it is only one source that it is coming from. You fought the battle and won last year and came out of it victorious.

The disciples encountered the great sign and wonder of Jesus multiplying the fish and bread to feed the multitude. They just left the presence of Jesus to go over on the other side; but when a contrary wind hit they panicked. We are in the same position, as we see God coming through for us times and times again, but when the abnormalities of life hit we begin to complain and question God. They have been in the position where they saw the miracles in the Potter's hand, the Master's hand of great incredible signs and wonders. They were exposed to a greater level of glory. The enemy sought ways for man to be derailed, that is, to lose his power and authority. Hold on a little while because your God is a consuming fire. I don't care what the enemy is doing.

I am a hard man to die, although I may be under the weather, but it is for a moment. Weeping may last for one night but joy is coming in the morning. Neighbour, why are you weeping like you have no hope? It is time to go over on the other side. I don't care what storm clouds may rise, winds may blow, I am going all the way. You are going all the way. There are some winds that have come to distract, kill and destroy you, but hold fast and never let go. I have seen God in his glory, in his power, authority and operation. Don't try to tell me that my God is dead, I just spoke to him today.

I don't know but have you ever been in a trouble that really rocked your ship? One where you feel like your heart is fluttering like a fowl? I can attest, I had an experience where for 5 days I was taking deep breaths with stress. Some contrary winds came to destroy me. Sometimes we have to sing, "Roll back the curtains of memories now and then; show me where you brought me from and where I could have been." At times when the pressure hits, you have to remind yourself of who you are and what God has said over your life. The devil cometh not, but to kill, steal and destroy. But God says I have come to give life and give it more abundantly. I shall not die but live and declare the works of my God. I shall live, life! Life! Life! Life! live again! Breathe again., sneeze again, laugh again.

The devil wants to shut down some people's sound, worship, hope, faith. He wants you to be disappointed and for you not to live again. This is for someone whom the devil has been messing with and the spirit of death is lurking after you. In this season I shall be like okro, I just slide out and rock out of every trouble. I am coming out. You are coming out. You are not going under, you are going! You are going! You are going! I am going! We are going! I feel somebody getting a break-through and shouting, "I am coming out! I am coming out! I am coming out! I am coming out!"

The wind that is blowing contrary carries all kinds of sounds, so you are hearing and seeing all manner of things. It looks like death! It looks like you are about to be destroyed but the God that you and I serve is coming through. We are not alone! You are not alone! You have some things on your mind that are troubling you, but you are not alone. If God is for you who can be against you? Jesus died for you. Jesus died for you. You are not alone. You are not alone. Declare I am not alone!

Although your ship may be rocking and the sails may be torn, you shall rest in the eyes of the storm. The storms of life are raging; contrary, boisterous winds are against you to backslide, stop going to church, get mad. But in the name of Jesus you shall live. Life! I shall live and not die in the name of Jesus. You shall rest in the eye of the storm.

The word of God declares, he that dwells in the secret place of the most high shall abide under the shadows of the Almighty (Psalm 91:1 KJV). Wake up, faithless generation of people. Do you think the word of God just came to make noise? It is sharper than any two-edged sword. You are going through your go through, now let go of compromise and cleave to righteousness and faith. I want to make an announcement, Jesus is alive and well, and He is able. Neighbour, let us rock out of this. It came to kill you but rock out!

Be determined, this will not kill me, and I am going over to the other side. Signs and wonders must follow you accordingly, decide in your mind, I must make it over to the other side. It took one night for us to have a roof on our church as we were using a tent that over time got dilapidated. Consequently, whenever it rained it fell on us like a strainer. The Lord constrained a sinner man, who builds the body of trucks, and had no time to waste, not even a day. He left his home before the break of day to come by the church to erect the zinc roof.

God lifted him up to work night and day so that we could have a habitable place to worship God. Some Christians miss it, as some rock will take people's place. We do not have to beg people every day to work for God, since His word must live and not die. It is not us who are worrying and saying, "What are we going to do?" God is in control.

When we looked up at the church roof, it was water pouring down on us under the tent. Weeping may endure for the night but the morning is coming, therefore, bit by bit we shall see great victory. Your present distress is a great testimony but some of you are too blind to see. If Christians do not rise up to build God's house, He can raise up sinners to build it. Your life looks a way now but if God is the captain of your ship, you cannot sink. The warfare is at 'fever pitch' and it's like you do not know what to do.

I am trying to let persons know that if you are serving God you are going to serve him in liberty. Grasp the concept of God. If He is rowing your ship it cannot turn over or sink. It was said that, the great titanic could not turn over but it sank, but If God is on your ship it cannot and shall never sink. There are some boisterous winds, contrary winds, and the spirit of death was on the titanic. Some of you feel the spirit of death, coldness on your feet; and you may feel like you are going under, and the stress causes you to be breathing and panting heavily. But before you visit a doctor to calm the nerve, try Jesus, He is the 'nerve calmer.'

Even nature itself responds to God. While they were in the

middle of the sea struggling with the heavy wind and the storm, Jesus showed up. Some of you owe some bills but Jesus is about to show up. You have pains in the body and God is about to bring healing. Your mind is under attack with mind binding spirit, Jesus is about to fix that. Some of you are going through the valley of the shadows of death and when you go to pray the enemy is showing you everything else. Your mind is all over the place. When you begin to focus on God, the enemy is showing you all the things you need to see, distracting you from being focused, so during the delivery of the word you are not paying attention, and some of you sleep. Once the bible is opened some people sleep. Once the word is alive some of you are fully distracted, or once the preacher starts preaching the story, the devil comes with his disruption. The devil is able to do that because you are too bound.

Do you know why the devil works for you to be bound? When God looses you, you are going to stay loosed and satan does not want you to be freed. Recently I was in my closet praying and some interfering thoughts started attacking my mind. The devil will give you ideas as well, and you will come out confused, and say it was God who spoke. If the devil starts to show you things and you begin to focus on them, you may misinterpret it and say it is God. Touch your head and say, "Let my mind be stayed on you Lord." You go in the presence of God and you can't define Him or identify His character. You start seeing your problems bigger than God's character. Right there that is defeat. But if you could grasp the concept of a supreme Counsellor, a Mighty Redeemer, the God of my salvation, the God that is able to deliver and give good success and breakthrough; then it is impossible to leave prayer miserable.

When you go before God to pray do not 'bomb rush' or bombard God with your problems, as that is your ego, and it is not going anywhere. When you can start seeing God in His infinite mercy, power, authority then you are getting somewhere. You must learn to caress God before you 'bomb rush' Him. When you start caressing God He starts dispensing His glorious power and presence. He begins to open your eyes to Him and you will exclaim, oh Glorious God I worship you! The God who is bigger than my problems. Now you are confident He is able to solve them.

Recently I was praying and I was tired. I said oh great God of the universe, the God that says let there be and there was. The same God who lays down the rudiments of this universe. The one who created Nichole and have her breathing. The one who commands the sun, the moon and the stars and they respond to Him. The one who is seated far above principalities and powers and spiritual wickedness in high places. By the time you say this the realms are open. Now identify Him in his infinite mercy, His compassion and His glorious presence. It will now build hope and faith and take away your problem immediately. Now your eyes are distracted from your problems, so you will see them no more; but you see the God who is bigger than your problems.

After that you realize the problems are not there to kill you, as you have now passed the realms of the killing and you are at the place of life eternal and you feel empowered. You are now big and mighty, because the anointing power is upon you. '*Touch a button nuh?*' Holy Ghost. Jesus! Glorious God! If nature responds to Jesus, then our problems must respond to Jesus.

Confession

Dear precious Father, I enter into your presence with my heart bow and ask that you wash and cleanse me with your efficacious blood. Forgive me of all the times that I lose hope, challenging your authority to take care of me. Oh God please give me the grace not to lose faith and hope in an atmosphere of miracles, signs and wonders in Jesus name, amen.

Day Twenty-One

Crossing Over into New Dimensions

Scripture: Joshua 3:1 -5

According to the scriptures, Joshua rose up early after the ordeal and evil report from the other spies. Now he was ready to cross over into that which the Lord was saying concerning him. At one point he was moving from Shittim to the Jordan. Shittim is another word for the acacia tree, which means regeneration, perseverance and integrity. Therefore, regenerate and persevere with your integrity, regardless of what the enemy is doing you will stand. Crossing over into the promise is basically crossing into the unknown. When they received the word it was an unknown place and they did not know what to expect. You can imagine receiving a promise, crossing over into it but you are not sure what to look for? They had great expectancy concerning the promise based on the level of the imagination of the description they received, therefore they were launching out into the deep with positive expectancies. When someone speaks to you, based on how they speak to you, you can possibly imagine what you should look forward to.

Israel camped by the Jordan, and at one point the feeling of hopelessness hit them. Accomplishment was the agenda and this was set before them. Although the expectancies were great based on what was described or promised to them, they now reached to a place where they felt hopeless. Have you ever been in a hopeless position although you are expecting greatness? While camping on the Jordan for three days, they received the word, launch out! This was the instruction they must obey; it was the only way they would have crossed over into that new and impossible dimension. There are times in our lives when things look hopeless, things seem far-fetched, you feel that you have been going like this for far too long, and you get weary by the day or hour. But you must remember there is a dimension that you must cross over into. You must position yourself with the resolve, that comes what may I must cross over.

Crossing over will not be easy, but I do not believe that God is a God who will kill his own deceptively. If God says "I am bringing you into new dimension" you cannot just sit down and wait, you have to get in His presence and seek His attention, listen for His instruction and do accordingly. The word of God declares that a lazy man must not eat; for by the sweat of our brow we shall eat bread, so I believe it is a sin for us to be lazy. The key component for the devil to use, is to attach the spirit of sleep and slumber to your laziness, and sleep and slumber bring stagnancy. If you cannot labour to be on your knees until you hear God, you are just lazy. Because lethargicness is already upon you, the devil adds a spirit of slumber and insomnia upon you. If the spirit of the snail is upon you, you cannot cross over into new dimensions, speed and acceleration must be upon you.

Many will say the Christian life is hard, but when we are a slave to our flesh it is harder. The flesh is fighting the spirit, it is at constant war between light and darkness, emotion and the spiritual realm. If I am going to achieve I must position myself and set my face like a flint and decide that I shall overcome. You can't get lazy in the middle of the war, and you can't receive coverage for the time that you stop moving. So many persons started out fervently in prayer and the devil hit them with discouragement, and before they knew it they get lazy. This is what the enemy needs to overcome you. Just imagine your spirit man is decreasing while your flesh is on the rise.

You are sleeping. Do you know why? It is because of your addiction to the internet, So many of you are so connected to the internet and when you don't have wi-fi service you are mad. You are connected to social media like: facebook, Instagram, tik-tok and you are infuriated by any form of disconnection. Similarly, that is how the devil is mad when he cannot pick you up. When you come off the radar of darkness, the devil is in a rage because he cannot access you, you are covered under the blood. When you are in this secure place the devil cannot come in your house and order you to sit in your sofa; neither can he lay in your bed and eat out your food. It is time to seek God for a new dimension.

God gave the instruction for Joshua to wait at the Jordan river, and Jordan looked impassable, but God is giving you an instruction how to approach it. How are you going to get the answer if you do not start seeking him? The fact that God promised you it does not mean you can be lazy and receive it, and It does not mean you should abort fasting and prayer. You may receive a word that you will be a prophet that does not mean you can't listen to your prophet anymore, so you need to sit down and learn and get instruction. If you go before your time you will be sick, derailed and go around in circles, so ask the

Lord to teach you how to wait.

New dimension is coming but you have to cross the Jordan, and go through the hungry days. Healing ministry is upon you but the fact that sickness is in your body, you have to command it to dry up. Sometimes some prophetic words are spoken over your life and the warfare intensifies. Financial crisis hit, contrary winds blow against your word, but wait on the instruction. Listen and wait on the instruction.

The bible said, Joshua was at a place of waiting; he waited on the instruction from God to cross over into the new dimension. In Joshua 1:8, "Let not the word depart from you; meditate on this word day and night and you will have good success and prosper." Let the word of my mouth and the meditation of my heart be acceptable in thy sight. Oh Lord my strength and my redeemer (Psalm 19:14) Thy word oh Lord have I hid in my heart that I will not sin against you, (Psalm 119:105 KJV) "Thy word is a lamp unto my feet and a light unto my path." It will guide, instruct, and show when, where and how to go (see Psalm 8:32).

God is not contrary; so He will not contradict himself, because His word says, before one jot or tittle of his word pass, heaven and earth will pass away. He said I honour my word above my name, hence if God says new dimension it is so. However, it requires that you have to come out of sleep, and slumber, and stay at the altar and watch the seasons. Lord what must I do, tell me God?

Recently I told someone that the grace they operate in, I did not receive it, because I see faith to another level. I see faith in foolishness where you have to remain faithful in some things that do not make sense. So I encourage you to maintain your position, persevere and wait; have faith, although the enemy is fighting, hold on even when one thing can be off and everything else goes wrong. Are you waiting at Jordan to cross over? Yes! You will have to wait. Your WAIT can become a WEIGHT, and a heavy one. Waiting on God can become a heavy burden, confusion, mayhem, discouragement, but do not be distracted, wait on the promise.

Although your wait is a burden, a weight, but wait! In waiting there can be mixed feelings, futility can become a result in that type of waiting. Disappointments can be a part of your waiting, but it is just for a while, so do not jump ship. Wait in and on God, and do not move before your time, since your promise is secured. Some people are telling you that you are out of your season and you missed some seasons, and that is not necessarily the truth. There are times that we can't walk in the blessing, because we are still dealing with ourselves. Some people can't get married as yet because they can't deal with themselves in one room, much more to have another person in their space.

Sometimes God has some weight of grace to pour on some people, but he cannot do it as yet, because pride, ego, arrogance, emotions are still alive. Some persons are so carnal, that if you are speaking with another person while they are passing, they assume you are gossiping about them. How are you going to deal with God's people when you can't deal with yourself? Paranoia begins to set in, and you are disturbed. The instruction is, Wait in God!

Joshua was well equipped and was in a position to lead the children of Israel, and so he took up where Moses left off. It was now time for him to go over the Jordan and it was overflowing its banks. The water came with a rushing, swelling tide and what was in front of them looked like a curse, it was impassable. The Lord spoke to them, but yet it looked impossible, far-fetched, and that is why without faith it is impossible to please God. How can I serve a God that I have not seen if I do not have faith?

It must mean that I have faith to believe in my heart that He is indeed a rewarder of them that diligently seek him. If the word does not come alive in my heart, I cannot live for God. Just imagine you are just getting prophetic words but no evidence. I recalled a season in my life I would be called out frequently by my pastor and received prophetic words that money was coming, although I was hungry. One night at the end of the service the bishop said, "you are going to be wealthy." I laughed like Sarah laughed because she was in an impossible situation, (Genesis 18:12 – 15).

Has anyone ever spoken over your life and you said me? You laughed because the situation does not look plausible? Old Sarah's breasts were shriveled by this, and her womb was barren, no hope of having a child. She was probably feeling a lot of pain and her husband who was 10 years older than her, an old man who lost his fire in the romance department. By this they may have been living like brother and sister only for companionship. The angel of the Lord showed up and said "your wife Sarah shall have a child, next year this time" (Genesis 18:10). She said, I lived for 90 years and I have never had a baby; is it going to happen now? There are times that God speaks to your situation and it becomes impossible because you are reasoning, rationalizing and calculating it, but God is greater than your calculator. He can match times and seasons; He is not confined to education or intellect. He can rise up a stone, and cause for the rock to worship when man refuse to worship him.

God will go down to the river and say rocks rise up! That is why we can never be into a position to say who is qualified for the call. God qualifies the called, just as Moses had a stutter and God called him. Moses had a reservation about speaking when he got the call, and God sent Aaron who had eloquence to accompany him, but God used Moses' mouth to speak. It does not matter what you can't do, that is why God can use you because you were not dependent on yourself. You have to depend solely on God to put the Word and the power in you.

A new dimension is coming but if you can't see it in the spirit you are not going to understand it. You can't lay down and play dead to see what God is up to now, so your faith has to be at the place to receive it. There were many signs and wonders that Jesus did, they manifested through the power of God, and at times He had to put the doubters outside. He could not work much miracles in His home town, because they knew Him by association. Isn't this the carpenter's boy who is now saying man must eat his flesh and drink his blood? We are going to stone you. Historically they knew Him and they said, "You can't speak to us."

Jesus had to go outside of His home town where faith was. I want to tell you today, that man may reject, revile you and say all manner of evil against you falsely for His name sake; but rejoice, weeping may last for a night but joy comes in the morning (Psalm 30: 5). Do not sell out your salvation or your God. Keep your faith high, lift up your head and shout hallelujah.

Jordan banks were overflowing, treacherous waters and it looked like a curse, and so it is that at times your blessing looks like a curse. How is it that the blessing looks like this? The devil wants you to get angry with God. A few spies crossed over before, but look at this great nation that has to cross over. There were blockages and obstacles that caused the mission to look impossible. Whatever impossible situation that you are going through God is the captain of the ship. Hallelujah! With Christ in the vessel you will be able to smile at the storm, and when the enemy comes in like a flood, the spirit of the Lord lifts up a standard (Isaiah 59:19) against that heavy water.

The Lord will remove your obstacle; He will give you break-throughs. The bible declares, "God remembered Noah." A well-known truth about darkness is that, it does not love light. Go ahead and declare that your obstacles that came in the wee hours of the morning, you will not block me in this season in Jesus Name. Without Faith it is impossible to please God. You ____________________ (insert your name) if you do not have faith you cannot please God.

Some people are blocked by witchcraft/obeah because they are feeding from other altars, but God says I am here to remove the obstacles. Some people's eyes are blinded by the gods of this world, and they take church for a ritual. Some are very religious, and when we come into His presence we have no expectation. God is a spirit, and they that worship him must worship him in spirit and in truth.

God knows your burdens and everything there is to know about you, and He knows your uprising and your down sitting. The bible says, if we make our bed in hell God will find us (Psalm 139:8), and it doesn't matter where we hide, we cannot hide from God. When you come in the presence of God, come with an expectation and do not leave with your burden. Where are you going to take it when you leave with it? Some persons come and sit down and wonder what time the sermon will be finished but you cannot curtail the move of the Holy Spirit. It is customary that when I reach close to church I start repenting, by saying Lord wash, cleanse and purge me.

Some persons have lost their fear for God when they come to the house of God, nonetheless the altar is dedicated to the God of our salvation to meet with Him. If we come in His presence chewing gum, we have lost the fear of God and He will not share his glory, and if we are children, we must be child-like. If we cannot humble ourselves as a child, we cannot be a part of the kingdom. We are not bound by the shackles of sin as Christians but we are prone to sin. I recall one day I was on the altar and consecrating myself and I was praying foolishness and the Lord rebuked me and said, "daughter do not allow your consecration to become a ritual?"

We must be different and intentional when we come before God, and acknowledge that He is your God. You cannot be a Christian and do not acknowledge God and get a break-through. If you are connected to God and you have an altar in your home, you will be sensitive in your spirit, and equally, Joshua had that connection, as he called the mighty men, the Priests who bore the ark. He said, "there is problem in Jordan, the waters look impassable." He instructed them to stand flat footed in the trouble. As Christians you say you love God but as soon as problems come you are not taking any calls and are gone into hibernation. You become suicidal, the truth of God is not in you, the devil is robbing your praise, peace and joy.

When troubles come you must be in the house. Look at your hypocrisy, when you are in your problem and distress if your best friend does not call or come and look for you, you have them off. You say, "Imagine I am in need of support and not even one of you care." Why have you backslidden from church when you were experiencing stress from the enemy? People will always talk, but do not be distracted by that, and come in the presence of God and touch heaven. Your relationship is unto God not man. If you are grumbling that you will not return to church because the pastor did not call you, that is the wrong attitude. Does that mean God has forgotten you? You are being a hypocrite as well, because you stopped praying and fasting. You are now complaining that you are tired now, so it proves that you were not genuine to God. What if God should treat you in that manner? Joshua had the weight on his shoulders, millions of people to cross over. You have a little school fee, rent to pay and you are behaving as if that is Jordan. Let us say that is your Jordan, what do you do when that bank has become the rushing aggressive water? You are hungry, and the old boyfriend found you and wants to re-kindle the fire, and you betray God for a morsel. It begs the question, why are you serving God?

If you serve the triune, self-existing God, the I Am that I Am, the bright and morning star, the one who said let there be and there was, the God who sits upon the circumference of the earth, and stretch out the clouds like a curtain. The one who sits far above principalities and powers. Demons and devils cannot oppress God, we do not wrestle against each other but against principalities and power, rulers of darkness and spiritual wickedness in high places. If He is sitting high above these things we must be convinced that we do not serve a puny 'wishy-washy' God. Why are you weeping as if there is no hope? If your heart does not belong to God, you will leave the church. But if you believe when Jordan banks are overflowing, He will not leave you to die.

God knew Israel by their name. God cannot be fooled, He knows your worship, and the times when you come to him. When you are absent He misses you. God knows you by the very strand of hair that is on your head. If you have confidence in him during Jordan's rushing river, then your faith will be lifted. Joshua did not call the engineers, workmen or educators He called those who were connected to the realms of the spirit. So you cannot use someone that is connected to the realms of the physical to address the spiritual. They will use psychology, the chemist calculates things, the anesthesian doctor will introduce the drugs for a surgery, and calculate the dosages based on a number of things concerning you: height, weight, age etc. Based on these factors they conclude what must be introduced to the body.

The mason knows how much cement to use to the requisite bags of sand, the baker knows how much baking powder to what measure of flour. Joshua who was spiritually aligned and connected, knew that he had to call the men who were connected to his God. He said stand up in the midst of the gushing Jordan River, man is no match to its current. But as they bare the ark they stood in the Jordan and the bible said, "Jordan river stood still." Your problems have to give way when the presence of the Lord touches it. Something has to happen, shift, change in the family, blood-line, community, finance, and salvation.

Some of you are walking around with some generation curses of divorce and college drop-outs. Shout, break it God! Uncommon favour, blessings, break-throughs come upon my life. Change my generation. Something has to change concerning my children, and church. Some of you desire to further your education but you are blocked because of financial lack. Break barriers, strongholds, generational curses, sleep, slumber in the name of Jesus Christ. God is here to give you life, so do not doubt God, trust Him. Get to know Jesus to a new dimension. Some people give excuses to be absent from the presence of God, ask the Lord for discernment to see what is happening in their life. See how the enemy is blocking them because their story, warfare is great.

In the name of Jesus Christ there is a breaking concerning you. You have cried for far too long, now every strong-hold that oppress you must break in the name of Jesus Christ, break by fire!. Every evil seed that were established against you must be broken in the name of Jesus Christ. God is a deliverer.

Joshua spoke to his children (Joshua 1:3), they were told to sanctify themselves and then they would be ready to cross-over. God asked these Priests to bear the ark and stand in the Jordan, and there was a 360 degree turn around. Declare that there will be a 360 degree turn around over your life, and destiny in the name of Jesus Christ the Son of the living God. I have been living in my season of testimony. Out of sleepless nights of prayer the Miracles of the Potter's Hand was birthed, and when a team of us started praying in the community the obeah men wanted to kill us. We were accused of stealing their members, consequently, at the same time Christians in the church ridiculed and accused us of being extra.

The witchcraft workers lossed their rest saying we must kill her. While we were having fasting on a Tuesday they had their meeting at the same time. The New Testament church where I worshipped was on a hill in close proximity to the obeah camp, In this rural community there were over 200 hundred persons in the fasting service. The iniquity workers found the facts they were looking for, a praying set of people. The evil man realized what was happening and decided that death is our portion. They set their tables and higher orders. Each time I would see my name on tables in the realms of the spirit, and everything that I saw was confessed to me recently. Also, our opposition was great within the church, the 'ratoons' who did not like to see growth, development and break-throughs had an issue with us.

Whatever the Holy Spirit is saying if you work with it you can never go wrong, therefore, do not be disturbed by religious fanatics, as they are bound by the spirit of religiosity and are false. They deny the power of God. Listen to the voice of God and you will be guided. I have been the pastor of Miracles of the Potter's Hand International and some people came to me with some ideas, I told them let me pray about it and if God does not speak I cannot do anything about it. If God does not instruct me how can I take it from you?

When the children of Israel were crossing over the red sea Miriam took a tambourine and she began dancing. She thought it was her high praises that did it. Upon this deductive reason she was comfortable to disrespect the man of God and was audacious to ask if Moses thought he is the only one that God speaks through. Miriam used her grace to be-little the servant of God. God said put them out of the camp. Some people will cause you to die in your process. You better listen to the voice of God. Jordan river overflowed but Joshua's faith in God gave him the courage to take up the ark and stand up in the water. Everything that was on the ground that was mushy, even those things dried up that the children of Israel would not slip and fall when they go across. God knows exactly what you need in this season.

The bible declares that as we keep our minds on God, (Joshua 1:8) and our actions in God we shall prosper and have good success.

Faith leads us into mega victories, that the law never did. Ask the three Hebrew boys when they decided not to bow, as they did not honour the law but their faith in God delivered them. Likewise, Hannah's pregnancy was the power of Faith, although Peninah mocked and jeered her, she went on the altar in her time of distressed. Meanwhile, the Priest misunderstood her and accused her of being drunk, and as a result, she moved into the ridiculous and then she received her miraculous. God wants to do some miraculous things but you must move into the ridiculous. Ask Ruth and even Naomi, as her three sons and husband were dead but Ruth cleaved by faith and there was a family to her.

In Joshua 3:7 KJV, the Lord declared unto Joshua, "This day will I begin to magnify thee in the sight of all Israel, that they may know that, as I was with Moses, so I will be with thee." I shall prosper, my children, family shall prosper, and every evil altar operating against my life shall be annihilated in the name of Jesus Christ. Some of you are living on some lands that are contaminated, so ask your pastor to pray over a bottle of olive oil and serve the land communion. There were some other things that used to serve on the land such as sugar and water for ancestral spirit. There are some active altars in our generational lineage; but we are Christian warriors and they must mash up, break, destroy! The community that I live in is riddled with witchcraft. We are not afraid of witches and warlocks, as we kick over bath pans, burn down mother flags and break their scepter and destroy their ranks and order. And Joshua said, "Hereby ye shall know the living God is among you, and he will without fail drive out from before you the Canaanites, Hittites, Hivites, Perizzites, Girgashites, Amorites and Jebusites." God shall destroy your enemies, haters who rise up against you. They shall be scattered by fire. They shall know that God is with you, they cannot kill you. You shall live and not die (Psalm 118:17).

There were many blows, darts, and arrows that came your way but you are still here. They desire that the church door be closed in this hour, but the devil is a liar. Every charismatic witchcraft that rise up against God's people shall die by fire. Touch not the Lord's anointed and do his prophet no harm. The enemies can only try but they cannot prevail, now in the name of Jesus Christ we declare war against the contender and every dart that comes against your head, we destroy it now. Do not get weary because God has called you to be different and he will speak to you. Every altar, bad mind, jealousy that rise up against you, we rip it up in the name of Jesus Christ. I declare war on your behalf.

Confession

Oh God my Father, here I am before you another time on bended knees. I cry out to you for mercies and grace and repent, where I have allowed the evil report of the enemies to intimidate me. You have not given me a spirit of fear but power and of love and of a sound mind. I trust you to take me over every Jordan situation and lift my faith that the battle is already won, in Jesus name, amen.

Bonus1: Day Twenty-Two

Victimized For God to be Capitalized

Scripture: Genesis 29

A victim can be defined in simple terms as someone who is treated unjustly, with cruelty and bad treatment. In the scripture we see Jacob running away from his father's house based on his mother's instruction, and he entered into the land of his generation where his family was. He reached his generation undisturbed, and made contact with his uncle Laban, his mother's brother. On the way by divine set up he met Rachel first. One may think that now he has reached the place of safety and was in his family's house, all would be well, but little did he realize that this would be a season of trauma, pain and agony. Many of us in this life, at one point or another we thought that we have overcame some challenges, attacks and were now settled. What we d not realize is, it was the beginning of something great in a negative way.

You are about to go through a struggle, a storm, the flood, and something is about to hit your life, that is enough to blow your mind negatively; but with Christ in our vessel we can now smile at the storm. This same Laban welcomed his nephew, and Jacob felt so good at uncle's house, Mommy sent him to go and look for a wife among family and not strangers; and now he is here, and nothing has changed. He felt he was in the place where he would have been victorious; but after a while Laban said unto him, "Although you are my nephew, you have to work for your wages."

Laban spoke to Jacob and asked him what is it that he wanted? Jacob said, "Let me have Rachel to be my wife," and Laban made a deal with Jacob. I believe Jacob was confident and he thought, "My problems are over because I am safely secured in my family's house." And the bible said, "Jacob began to weep and he kissed Rachel, for now he has found his wife in a strange land." I don't know if some of you know what it means to be in a strange land. See I have been in that position, and you may need pots and pans, spoons and fork. Do not believe that when you leave one place and run to another that it is going to be easy. It was just the beginning of sorrows for this man. Your weeping season shall be turned into your leaping season in Jesus name.

Some of you have been abandoned and rejected, while others have some family members that you do not want to have anything to do with them. But I would like to say to you today, hold on to your victory because you will not be in the position of a victim forever. I declare to you that victory is on the way, and it does not matter what they did to you, victory shall happen for you.

Regardless of the cruelty that was done to you, if you hold on to the unchanging hands of God, you shall overcome. Jacob worked seven years, at hard labour for his wife, and he was excited to get Rachel. When the seven years were expired, he said to his uncle, "May

I have my wife?" because I have labored. I am not sure who has short-changed you but God is about to do exploits on your behalf; so I charge you, do not fight this battle, it belongs to the Lord. He will take you through, so keep your heart pure and clean, and do not get bitter. Let go of unforgiveness because your God is a consuming fire and He is about to expose some snakes.

Some of you have been held captive for so long because there are some snakes under the grass. They pretend to be with you but they would do everything to kill you. But declare that you shall not die! They thought you were dead but you are 'dead and wake,' a hard man to die. You should have killed me when I was outside of Christ but now I am under the blood you cannot kill me. There are some who do not know who God's people are, and do not understand what it means when God placed you in the womb.

The word of God concurs, that "Before you were placed in the womb I knew you and ordained you a prophet to the nation" (Jeremiah 1:5 – 6). Some persons see you but they do not understand what is on your life. It is the grace that is upon you, whether they are jealous, bad mind, covetous they can't harm you because there is a glory on your life and hell cannot stop it. It is a run-away train. The devil can come against you with full force but you are as slippery as okra. When the pressure hits you, what was the word that God spoke over your life? Hell has nothing on this word.

When God says you are anointed it is so, and all shall see the manifestation of what he has placed on your life. The anointing will fight for you, and protect you, and if you are favored, favour isn't fair. God is the glory and the lifter up of your head, thus whatever some people try against you to hurt you it will not work. If they try to stop you it will only backfire in their faces, therefore, they can't get you out of the race. Although there are obstacles in your way you are still running your race, so keep running. Stay at the altar, fast and pray. There are conspiracies, cliques against you but you are covered.

The anointing is bearing fruit in your life. Are you a warrior, and do you know how to guard your territory, rip up, mash up, tear up and scatter by fire? No mix up, tie up, tangle up powers can touch you, since God is a shield for you in the North, South, East and West. The storm is coming but God will protect you. Do not be afraid, if God is for you who can be against you (Psalm 27), Which devil, fanatic, bad mind people can stop you? You do not need to physically defend yourself, just take it to the Lord in prayer.

Every day the wicked thinks about being wickeder, and God says I am angry with the wicked. Sadly, there are some wicked and jealous church people, which does not make the warfare external but internal (Psalm 55). Many times we are looking outside for the enemy and we are deceived and losing the battle; because we are looking in the wrong place. If the Holy Spirit uses you to do something, the spirit of jealousy rises up against you. As God opens your financial womb there is conspiracy against you. In some seasons you are dealing with charismatic witchcraft.

When Jacob said the time has come it is my time to shine, his uncle Laban backed the scale and did not give him his just weight, similarly, this is how you have been victimized many times in your life. I encountered so much jealousy when I just got saved, by way of some criticizing the anointing on my life and calling it fake. Some accused me of being an obeah worker but God sent his re-assurance that He placed that grace on me. Also understand that some people will misunderstand you. Have you ever been in a position where you are traumatized, and you can't take anymore, and subsequently, everyone who comes around you, you begin to screen them? If it had not been for Jesus, you would have lost your mind.

You do not need man's approval, since man will elevate you today for something and put you down tomorrow. When the enemy comes in like a flood the spirit of the Lord will lift up a standard (Isaiah 59:19 KJV). Let me confess that I was the child who gave my mother the most heart ache, therefore, when I should have been in school I was at my boyfriend's home. But there was a great purpose on my life, not even I knew that fact. I recall I would oftentimes pray to escape a beating and my prayers would be answered. My purpose was being incubated in the womb of my destiny.

I am here to declare that you will give birth, since what you are carrying is not ordinary; so do not get discouraged, carry your child to full term. The time will come when you have to push out purpose, and destiny. Signs and wonders will follow you and no one will be able to victimize you anymore. You are going all the way, and you are crossing over. I am speaking to you, Mr/Mrs dead and wake. Man and woman of purpose. Annihilate some things, set your face like flint, and stop crying, do not die in your pain, nor give up on God. Where were they when you were on your way to hell and the rope was around your neck but God rescued you? Your harsh circumstances in life were designed to victimize you but God has capitalized on them to give you a great and bright future so that He will be glorified. You are not a victim you are a victor. Stay blessed.

Confession

Heavenly Father, I come to you in the Mighty name of Jesus Christ of Nazareth, I confess oh Lord that I was traumatized by my victimization in this life. It was hard to trust and let go and let you have your way. Now I come to my full senses that it was all for your glory. Oh God please forgive me for falling short of the standard you set for me when I slowed down because of the critics. Strengthen me oh God, wash me, purge me, purify me and cleanse me from all unrighteousness. Lord give me renewed strength and grace to continue running the race in Jesus mighty name.

Part 2
Prophetic Acceleration

"Thou shalt also decree a thing, and it shall be established unto thee: and the light shall shine upon thy ways."

Job 22:28 KJV

Every man has the power to change the course of his destiny if he would open his mouth and speak of those things which are not as though they were. God knows His authority and so he opened his mouth and declared, "Let there be and there was!"

Just by exercising your authority in the earth and emphatically declaring these prophetic decrees mixed with faith, you will encounter divine acceleration in every area of your life.

Day 1: Declaration

1. May ___________________________ (your name) decrease while Christ increase in me. My tongue must be subjected to the authority of the Lord Jesus Christ. My tongue is the pen of a ready writer, it shall write everything that God is saying in this season.
2. I am here not to be ordinary but I shall be more than a conqueror through Jesus Christ. I shall be talked about. Why? Because the Spirit of the Lord is upon me.
3. I decree and declare no limits! No boundaries! Every limitation that is upon me I break it by fire!
4. Oh Lord, I decree and declare that my Faith is on fire and I believe without wavering that which I desire in this season is mine.
5. In the name of Jesus Christ I decree and declare that my Faith shall silence every boisterous wind as I walk on them.
6. Oh Lord, I activate my Faith and authority and I command an acceleration of release in the realms of the spirit, of every wealth and prosperity that were held up for my ancient generation to be dispensed unto me and my generations now, by fire.
7. Give ear oh heavens and respond oh earth to my prophetic voice, let the secret treasures hidden in secret places be

released unto me now in Jesus Name.

8. I speak to every seeming impossible situations in my life by the authority of Jesus Christ and I command you to align with the will and purpose of God for my life and destiny now in Jesus Name.
9. I decree and declare that the best things belong to me to eat, live, wear, drive, spend, and have in Jesus Mighty name.
10. Oh Great God Almighty who stretch out the heavens like a curtain, may you stretch out my Faith to ridiculous proportions to believe you for the miraculous in this season.

Day 2: Declaration

1. I will shout to God for the joy of my salvation, I sing praises unto Him and now victory is in my cup because God has delivered me from my strong oppressor.
2. Now my father, by the blast of your nostril the enemy must change before me by your power.
3. I now declare my eyes shall see, I shall testify of His tangible power. Even the sea must dry up at the blast of His nostrils.
4. By executive order I declare my feet shall walk on dry ground. Every difficulty that caused my feet to slip shall respond to the fire of Jesus Christ by drying up, in Jesus Mighty name.
5. I decree and declare my going out and my coming in shall be compact with the joy of the Lord in Jesus mighty name.
6. I decree and declare in this season that my testimonies are very sure. The mighty God, is solving all my issues in this season in Jesus Mighty name.
7. Father, break in pieces oh Lord my contenders, my afflictor, my heritage blocker. Lord laugh at the hand that come against my inheritance. The Lord grant me the desire of my heart in this season in Jesus Mighty name.
8. Oh Lord my Father, let not the wicked triumph over my life, let the length of their days be shortened because you are angry

with the wicked every day.

9. Lord I decree and declare rest upon your beloved in this season, may there be a foundational change on my behalf, shake into place every victory that belongs to me in Jesus Mighty name.

10. I call forth rest upon my life today by the power of God. Rest from my adversity. God my Father in this rest, may you dig with speed the pit for the wicked, my adversary. Let judgment come upon them unaware, in Jesus Mighty name.

Day 3: Declaration

1. Oh my God, all of my trust is in your Father, let not those who hate me triumph over me in Jesus Mighty name.
2. Father, I now ask that you guide my walk with you in this journey. May your knowledge enlarge me, I declare I shall be as established through your mercies and my enemies will be ashamed and will turn back from pursuing me, because they are defeated.
3. Father, consider the abject that gather themselves against me, how many they are, their cruelty against me. Consider how much they hate and plot against me, and now oh Lord grant them according to their work. Give them what they worked for by the blast of your anger, in Jesus mighty name, Amen.
4. Father, by your authority, redeem Israel oh Lord, from all troubles. Let integrity preserve and establish me by fire, in Jesus Mighty name.
5. Father your voice is upon the water, your voice is powerful, your breaketh strongholds. May your voice speak to my life with power and clarity in this season.
6. And now my Father may you set my feet in a large place, deliver me with speed for thou art the rock of my fortress, my strong tower.
7. Oh Lord let my deliverance come in your righteousness, let joy

flow from my belly because you have remembered me, in Jesus Mighty name.

8. Lord, let your righteous anger be lifted on my behalf, may you turn my mourning into dancing. May you take all my bulrushes and gird me with gladness. Oh Lord my God, I will give thanks to you forever, because you are good to me.

9. God my Father, I now speak and declare, the pit of the grave shall long for me, I will rejoice in thy salvation perpetually. I cannot praise you in thy grave, so now my father take away every garment of grief and grant me the garment of praise and worship in Jesus Mighty name.

10. Oh my Lord, may you bow down your ear to my cry, Lord let not the enemies triumph over me, pull out the evil that they have laid out against me. Let me not be a reproach among my neighbor. Let me never be ashamed, rescue me with speed in Jesus Mighty name.

Day 4: Declaration

1. I hereby decree and declare that in the mighty name of Jesus Christ that I have legal rights in the earth, to bind on earth and it shall be bound in heaven, I have the authority to bind on earth and heaven responds with speed.
2. For my God has given me authority over all the powers of the enemy and I am empowered to speak to unclean spirits and they must obey and flee.
3. I have the authority to cleanse the leper, heal the sick, raise the dead. I ____________________(your name) have the authority in the earth because of your authority in heaven. Victory is my portion in Jesus name.
4. Oh Lord thou hast beset me behind and before, your mighty hands are upon me, may this be perpetually in Jesus Mighty name.
5. Oh God my Father, let your true vine be embedded upon my life, in Jesus mighty name.
6. Lord, you said the waters will not overflow me, the fire shall not consume me, let your covenant stand for me in the day of my calamity and prevail against the judge of destruction and give me a loud testimony in Jesus name.
7. Father I thank you for the season of newness in my life, I shall behold and see your great and mighty hand.

8. Oh Lord my Father, you have chosen me in the furnace of my afflictions, now Lord establish me with your glory, in Jesus Mighty name.

9. Father, may you avenge Zion, feed them that oppress me with their own flesh, let them be drunken with their own blood and all flesh shall say, surely the Lord has remembered Zion.

10. Father I thank you for my registration, surely there is no bill of divorcement for me. Let no iniquity prevail against my freedom, let not transgression prevail over my victory in you. But now oh Lord let the scepter of my evil creditor be totally annihilated. The God of my salvation has redeemed me, Hallelujah!

Day 5: Declaration

1. I decree and I declare in this season, every red sea condition shall be dried up, by the blast of the nostril of the Lord, in Jesus mighty name.
2. Le the troubles of the waters cover all my enemies, so none shall be left in Jesus mighty name.
3. Oh my Father, every Dathan, every Abiram that have risen up against me, may the earth now open up and swallow them, in Jesus name.
4. Oh my Father, I decree and declare that uncommon favour shall be attached to my life and prevail over my generation perpetually in the mighty name of Jesus.
5. May the favour of God locate me through my faith like Esther and all who look upon me, shall favour me, in Jesus mighty name.
6. Oh God of vengeance, by your super-natural power let the heart of mine enemies become so hard, that you will be honoured upon the host of my contenders and all those who seek my life to destroy it in Jesus mighty name.
7. Now, I decree and declare a separation between my camp and that of mine enemies, when it is the cloud of light for me, it shall be great clouds of darkness for my enemies. Let them stumble in the dark and confused in the web that they have

set up for me, in Jesus mighty name.

8. Every red sea that have come to devour me let the mighty hand of God begin to exercise in his infinite power, and let the strength of His nostrils blow and cause for this destruction to reverse, in Jesus mighty name.

9. Lord, may day break come on my behalf and let the last watch of the night come victorious for me, may you look down from your pillar of fire at the enemy and may you throw them into confusion, those who come to scatter me may you scatter them by your fire, in Jesus mighty name.

10. Oh Lord, in this I know you favoured me, I have seen the blast of your hand, even in the hottest battle you have given me peace! Surely I confess that the Lord has been good to Zion, Amen!

Day 6: Declaration

1. Father in the Mighty name of Jesus Christ, I decree and declare that every evil decree that is set up against my life through governmental authority, shall be dumbfounded, back-fire with the very destruction that they have set up for me, in Jesus mighty name.

2. You evil contender, contending with the righteous, I decree and declare that the spirit of the Lord is upon me in the east to stand for His glory.

3. Arise my Father and spare me from the clutch of the wicked one, my soul shall not see corruption because I trust in thee.

4. Father, may you open your eyes to the kingdom that has risen up against my life, just as you opened your ears to my supplication and now my father deliver with empirical evidence.

5. Lord, can I run away from the wicked that bend their bow against me, the arrows that they sent against your upright in heart? Look and see them Lord, do not turn away in the day of my affliction, in Jesus mighty name.

6. Let the spirit of excellence that is upon me now bring forth and produce, so that those who laugh first shall laugh last, in Jesus mighty name.

7. Every evil angel that comes from the pit of hell let the angel of

the Lord chase them and beat them to dust, let there be ashes to ashes and dust to dust for mine enemies in Jesus name.

8. My God, may you send your angel and shut the mouth of every lion and let them not hurt me, my children, my household, my generation in Jesus mighty name.

9. Oh Lord, let the king's command be in my favour in Jesus mighty name.

10. I decree and declare that the Lord my God shall send assigned angels with me, in the way of my success, in Jesus Mighty name.

Day 7: Declaration

1. Father, in the Mighty name of Jesus I decree and declare more of you, let the shadows of your glory be upon me perpetually, in Jesus name.
2. Oh my Lord, you are my shield, my fortress, my God and my strong tower, in you will I continue to trust, in Jesus Mighty name.
3. I will declare the name of the great and terrible God among the heathen because he is a great God and to be feared above all other gods.
4. Great and terrible God, Majesty and Honour are before thee, strength and beauty are in your sanctuary. My God your lightening lighteth the whole world, the earth saw it and trembled.
5. Let the fields be joyful at your presence, Lord let the trees rejoice at your presence. Let the trees melt like wax at your presence. Lord let the whole world tremble at your presence and let your glory never leave me.
6. Oh Lord my God, because you are standing on my behalf, drive out all destiny stoppers, blockers and destroyers in Jesus mighty name.
7. Oh Mighty God, my strong deliverer, deliver me from all Hittites, those governmental authorities that block purpose. I

command them to hear the voice of the Lord and come under subjection, through the power and authority of Jesus Christ. Lord give me victory over them even now.

8. I break the ranks, sceptre, spade and spear of the Hittites that flow from their authority and by the mighty power of Jesus Christ victory is in my cup, in Jesus Mighty name.

9. Father! I pray by your fire may you burn, cancel and dismantle every Jebusite spirit that come against my assignment with the crippling spirit of fear. Oh Lord may you burn that hitman, you who come to defile my body, mind and spirit. I will not be a victim because the Lord my God is fighting for me in Jesus Mighty name.

10. I shall rejoice in this season, my next level is here, because my face to face with God supercede the spirits that come to distract me in the name of Jesus.

Day 8: Declaration

1. Father, in the mighty name of Jesus, I decree and declare more of you. Let the shadows of your glory be upon me perpetually, in Jesus name.
2. Oh Lord my God I break, cancel and dismantle the attacker of self-confidence, everything that comes to infiltrate my thoughts with negativity to derail my assignment, they are already defeated in Jesus name.
3. Oh my Lord, you are my shield, my fortress, my God and my strong tower, in you will I continue to trust in Jesus mighty name.
4. I command in the Name of Jesus, a breaking of every yoke that comes with strongholds for me to fail, I pull on Joshua 3:9 - 10. O come near all warriors who are destined for victory, the Lord thy God shall drive out all your enemies from around you without failing. All the Perizzites, Girgashites, Amorites, Jebusites, Hivites and Canaanites, that is your portion in this season, in Jesus Mighty name. Amen.
5. I decree and declare that I now live in the over flow. Oh Lord, may my enemies who come with slandering and gossiping to murder with their tongue and murmur against me like Aaron and Miriam, may you hear them oh Lord and answer their prideful and envious spirit. May you reward them according to their Amorite Spirit and now grant me the courage to prevail,

in Jesus Mighty name.

6. Oh Lord I will not be a stiff-necked mourner to the Great and terrible God, but as a child I shall be rightly aligned and positioned, because the Lord is for me, victory is mine in Jesus Name.

7. Oh my Heavenly Father, may you give me a face to face with you, may your glorious presence prevail over me perpetually, O My Lord those who look on my downfall and seek to laugh, mock and jeer me, may they die wasting in Jesus Name.

8. I will declare the name of the great and terrible God among the heathen because he is a great God and to be feared above all other gods.

9. Great and terrible God, Majesty and Honour are before thee, strength and beauty are in your sanctuary. My God your lightening lighteneth the whole world, the earth saw it and trembled.

10. I declare your presence shall be upon me in this season; Let your presence give me access to bind princes, their authority and to teach senators in Jesus Mighty Name.

Day 9: Declaration

1. I declare this day that a land flowing with milk and honey is my portion in Jesus mighty name.
2. Father, as your word declares in Psalm 1, that you know the way of the righteous, let your establishment be upon the righteous now in a mega way. May you stretch your blessing perpetually upon me by executive order in Jesus mighty name.
3. Father, I decree and declare I shall delight myself in you oh Lord. May you grant me the desires of my heart in Jesus mighty name.
4. I am the righteousness of God. I shall rest in the cleft of his rock, I will be content in my God and will not fret about those who wickedly plot against me in Jesus mighty name.
5. Remember me oh Lord with your favour let me see the good of your chosen that I may rejoice in gladness, that I may glory within thine inheritance in Jesus mighty name.
6. My father I decree and declare I will not be like my ancestors, give me knowledge and understanding for this journey, upon my eyes to your wonders let me always remember the multitude of your tender mercies let your mighty power be known through me in the mighty name of Jesus.
7. May the earth be open at my Dathan and swallow up the envious Abirams and company for my sake in Jesus mighty

name.

8. Lift up your hands against the murmuring camp of Abiram and company. Overthrow in the wilderness of your wrath in the mighty name of Jesus Christ of Nazareth.

9. Let the countenance of your glory oh God my father, hide me in the cleft of your rock in the mighty name of Jesus.

10. May the God of my salvation command the clouds from above on my behalf. Open the heaven and cause for the rain to pour down manna upon me and my generation so we can eat, let us eat the corn of heaven.

Day 10: Declaration

1. I decree and declare that whenever the wicked gather to mention my name, the power of the Holy Ghost shall answer this gathering in Jesus mighty name.
2. Oh Lord, let your fire visit the root of any evil family member of mine, and burn their altars and destroy their evil mandate in Jesus Mighty name.
3. I declare I shall have double for my shame. I shall receive everlasting joy, this is my portion in Jesus Name.
4. Everything that the enemy has stolen from me through dreams, I must receive double in Jesus Mighty name.
5. I declare that my spirit man is equipped and is aligned for victory, even in my sleep. I shall be victorious in Jesus Powerful Name.
6. Father, in Jesus Mighty name, according to Job 33:15 - 17, even in dreams and vision, in the department of my sleep, my ear shall be opened to be sealed with your instruction.
7. When you lay me down at night, I shall not be afraid, my sleep shall be sweet, for your ministering angels shall encamp round about me, I thank you Lord that you have given your beloved rest, in Jesus Christ Mighty name.
8. St. Matthew 18:18 has given me the authority to bind in the

earh and it shall be bound in heaven, to loose on the earth and it shall be loosed in heaven. I bind territorial powers, witchcraft forces and every evil mission operating in my location in Jesus Mighty name.

9. Let your people be joyful in glory Lord, let them sing upon their bed your highest praises shall flow from the mouth of the righteous. Let there be an execution upon the camp of my contenders in Jesus Mighty name.

10. I have the authority over the heavens to bind their kings with chains and their nobles to execute judgment upon thine enemies, in Jesus Mighty name.

Day 11: Declaration

1. You my Father are a shield and buckler for all those who wait upon you. May you save the afflicted, remember our troubles and bring down the high and mighty that wage war against your blood, in the name of Jesus Christ.
2. Oh Lord my Father, may you enlighten my dark path, channel and troublesome waters that are coming at me from evil foundation of my contenders. May you rebuke the strong force of their customs by the blast of your nostrils in Jesus Mighty name.
3. The horn of my salvation is exalted, my deliverer, my buckler, my high tower, hide me in the day of my distress as you bow down the heaven.
4. Lord preserve me in Jesus Mighty name. Let your goodness be extended to my generation and the excellent spirit that is upon me, live in the portion of what you pour out for me to drink. Let the sorrows of mine enemies be multiplied and those who bow to other gods be cut off without remedy.
5. Let the fields be joyful at your presence, Lord let the trees rejoice at your presence. Let the trees melt like wax at your presence. Lord let the whole world tremble at your presence and let your glory never leave me. Lord may you go with me perpetually, in Jesus Name.

6. Oh Lord, as you answered your priests: Moses, Aaron and Samuel who call upon thy name and you answered them, I declare when I call upon your name, you will answer me speedily, in Jesus Name.

7. Father, in the mighty name of Jesus I declare as you spake to Israel in the pillar of the cloud, so shall you speak to me and answer me. I declare that your ordinances and testimonies shall be in my mouth perpetually in Jesus mighty name.

8. I declare your presence shall be upon me in this season. Let your presence give me access to bind princes and the authority to teach senators wisdom in Jesus name.

9. In this season, Lord may you increase me greatly, strengthen me oh Lord, increase my portion in Jesus mighty name.

10. Let the cloud be a covering upon me, and your fire give me light in every dark destructive set up of my enemies in Jesus mighty name.

Day 12: Declaration

1. I decree and declare that the God of Shadrach, Meshach and Abednego is fighting for me. He is answering my every request for his presence even in the hottest battles in Jesus Mighty name.

2. In this season may you show up and change the visage of my enemies. Disappoint them, oh Lord my father and every burning fiery furnace, that is carefully lit to consume me let the enemies perish in them, in Jesus Mighty name.

3. Oh Lord, may you open the eyes of those that set up traps against my life, let them see my deliverance. Let them know that the God of my salvation will neither sleep nor slumber in Jesus Mighty name.

4. Lord I thank you that you are my helper, thank you that you have hasten my escape from every windy storm and the tempest that come to beset me. I thank you that I am drinking from my cup of victory, in Jesus name, Amen!

5. Every evil Chaldean that rose up against me because of that evil judge, may you take away every good things from their hands with a mighty whirl-wind; et them know that my God is fighting for me. My God scatter them by your fierce anger in Jesus Mighty name.

6. Consuming fire, sweet perfume, defend me oh God from them that rise up against me; from the workers of iniquity and bloody men, in Jesus Mighty name.

7. Oh Father, may you see all those who run to prepare themselves as a sacrifice against my life. Awake to my help and judge those who found no fault in me but continue to oppress me in the Mighty name of Jesus.

8. My Father! My Father! Awake to my help, oh Lord of Host, God of Israel, God of vengeance, visit the heathens and be not merciful to their wicked transgression of the enemies.

9. God of vengeance you are my defense, my iron pillar, my brazen wall. I will perpetually sing, praise and worship unto you my God, you are merciful unto me all the day long, God of thunder.

10. Out of my distress you have heard my vows. The evil consultations of the enemy have scattered against me, their plots have ravaged the humble, let your everlasting light be my portion perpetually, in Jesus Mighty name.

Day 13: Declaration

1. Father, in the mighty name of Jesus as you stilleth the noise of the seas and the noise of their waves, I declare you shall quiet the tumultuous applause of those who gather together against me in Jesus mighty name.
2. Every disorderly crowd that wage war against my success, receive lava upon your head by the wrath of the power of God in Jesus mighty name.
3. Father, see those who chase me in the spirit, may your hand shoot at them, with your flying arrow let the suddenly wound them with your incurable wound, in the mighty name of Jesus.
4. Every flattering tongue that rise up against me with a venomous curse, oh Lord let their own tongue fall upon themselves all the days of their lives, in Jesus mighty name.
5. By executive order, every stronghold that stand against my destiny must come down, as they lay private snares and connive their evil matters. As they say who can see their evil against me, may you diligently visit them by the wrath of your angel in Jesus mighty name.
6. God you are my Rescuer, may you deliver me from my strong enemies and from those who rose up against me and those who hate me without a cause.

7. Oh God my father, may you rescue me according to my righteousness, even according to the cleanness of my hands in Jesus mighty name.

8. Father my deliverer you are the God who delivers me. May you gird me with strength, may your might give me hinds feet, cause for me to stand even in the most slipperiest path. I shall stand victoriously because you shall direct my path.

9. Let the shield of thy salvation be my inheritance. Let there be an overtaking of great success upon me as I pursue those with the baton of victory in Jesus mighty name.

10. God of my salvation, be exalted in the hour of my victory. Because you have girded my loins to fight and caused for my hands to war, even when my contenders were too strong for me, you caused for me to drink from the cup of victory.

Day 14: Declaration

1. My Father, my Father, the fact that I was placed in the womb of my mother, it means you are accountable and you have a plan for my life, before expulsion from the womb.
2. Now my God, whatever you have intended for me, help me not to miss it in this life. In the name of Jesus.
3. Lord teach me the ways and help me to understand, laws and precepts and principles of your kingdom. Help me and give me intelligence, spiritually to overcome the wiles of the devil and help me to be victorious through your blood in Jesus name.
4. Oh Lord, I decree and declare that the mind of Christ is upon me, I think victory at all times.
5. I decree and declare that as I shift position and raise my standard, every hand of sabotage against my life, must wither and die by fire now, in Jesus Christ mighty name.
6. Oh Lord I decree and declare that I am focused with a strong belief that, my next level is here. I will not panic because you have not given me a spirit of fear, but of power, love and a sound mind.
7. I decree and declare that every goliath situation that came to intimidate me, I conquer them through the power of your word. I quit myself like man and I fight because victory is in

my cup.

8. I decree and declare that I am a mighty warrior in the earth. I fight from a place of victory, because my hands are trained to war and my fingers to fight, in Jesus mighty name.

9. Oh Lord, I cannot be defeated, I raise my standard to that of Jehovah El-gibbor and I war in the heavens, and reject the little and claim the super-super, miraculous abundance in Jesus Mighty name.

10. Let the blessings of the Lord locate me by fire, by force, because I am unstoppable, I am untouchable, un-moveable under the order of Jesus Christ.

Day 15: Declaration

1. I decree and declare that every spirit of tradition that attached itself to me is now broken and annihilated by fire in the Mighty name of Jesus Christ.
2. Oh Mighty Everlasting God, I declare that every trouble in my life that is out of control, recede by the mighty power of God's word, that when I pass through the waters you will be with me and the rivers will not overflow me. When I pass through the fire I shall not be burnt neither shall the flames kindle upon me. Therefore no trouble can drown me, back up! Back up! In Jesus name.
3. I decree and declare that the anointing of the trouble moving grace is upon me, for though I walk through the valley of the shadows of death, I will fear no evil.
4. I decree and declare that God's covenant of promise is upon me, I shall lack no good thing, I am the head and not the tail, my water is blessed, my food basket is blessed, my womb is blessed, I am prosperous and no devil in hell can stop it!
5. I decree and declare that my mount Ararat is here, my seasons of frustration and set-backs are gone with the flood, it is a new season and I have every reason to give God a mighty shout of hallelujah.
6. Arise oh Mighty God, give Zion rest, let the ark of thy strength

be upon me perpetually in Jesus Mighty name.

7. Arise my Father, let me see the goodness of your Mighty hand concerning my desire, let rest be my portion; and your abundance of provision saturate me. May the satisfaction of more than enough be my washpot (meaning the vessel in which the conqueror's feet are washed) in Jesus Mighty Name.

8. Oh my Father, Arise by the blast of your anger, stretch forth your hand against them that hate Zion, let them be as the grass that withereth by the scourge of the sun, in Jesus Mighty name.

9. Arise oh God and deliver me from the hands of evil men; let your preservation be upon me and save me from violence, in Jesus Mighty name.

10. Every wicked spirit that plotteth against me and gnasheth with their teeth, I declare the wrath, the judgment of your anger will spin after them in Jesus Mighty name.

Day 16: Declaration

1. Neighbour, stand still in the deep waters. Do not get distracted, excited but be still and you shall know that the living God is above you and that you will not fail to drive out your enemies with the help of God.
2. I decree and declare that there is a divine announcement in the realms of the spirit concerning me, that the Almighty God has released a rainbow of promise that the troubles of yesterday cannot affect me today, afflictions will not arise a second time in Jesus Christ Mighty name.
3. Oh Lord, my Mighty battle-axe, may you arise and hew down with speed, every wicked contending enemy against my destiny, surprise them with a fatal blow to the head until they are dead in Jesus Christ name.
4. My Father, my Father, let the clock of victory come upon my life in this season in the Mighty name of Jesus.
5. Father, let the clock of judgment begin to take on my persecutors, let the time of your execution come up on all my contenders by executive order in Jesus Mighty name.
6. I decree and declare that those who lit a fire against my life, shall be caught in that same trap of fire; I now declare that they shall be bottled in the smoke, consumed by their own evil demise, in Jesus Mighty name.

7. I decree and declare that the proud who dug an evil pit for me, shall experience everything that was set out for me, let destruction come upon them unawares in Jesus Mighty name.

8. And now oh Lord, unto thee do I lift up my head, let not mine enemies triumph over me; let them die a miserable death waiting on my demise in Jesus Mighty name.

9. My Father, I now declare that the rod of the wicked shall never rest upon the lot of the righteous in Jesus Mighty name.

10. I decree and declare that my help is in the God of my salvation who made the heaven and the earth, my enemies shall never have dominion over me because my backative is in the Most High God.

Day 17: Declaration

1. The impossible shall become possible. I shall cross over the waters. As God gave it to Moses and did it to Joshua, so shall he do it for me.

2. I now decree and declare that the borders are extended, let there be an expansion upon my life in the mighty name of Jesus, I am bless! I am bless! In the city, field, in my going out, in my coming in, I am bless.

3. My God will make a show of principalities and powers triumphing over them. Oh Lord make a show over my enemies, laugh at them and give me victory in Jesus name.

4. God has his hands on me and they can't take it off. I rise to the occasion and understand that I am a mighty warrior. No devil in hell can stand against me.

5. I declare that I delight myself in the Lord, Oh Father grant me my desire in Jesus Mighty name.

6. Father, I decree and declare that the abundance of joy and peace shall be my portion because the inheritance of the righteous is upon me in Jesus Mighty name.

7. My Father, let your diligence consider all my afflictions and let an abundance of restoration be my victory portion in Jesus Mighty name.

8. I decree and declare that the hand of my God shall bring forth His righteousness because your judgment shall be as the noonday in Jesus Mighty name.

9. Oh Lord, victory is in my cup I will not go under, I shall rise as a warrior, I shall rise as a Christian. I am extra-ordinary, the mind of Christ is in me. The greater is in me.

10. In the name of Jesus Christ I shall rise, I am the head and not the tail. I believe I am a child of the King. I am victorious through the power of my Lord. I am not alone I belong to Jesus.

Day 18: Declaration

1. Father, in this life, in this land, I need a double and a triple grace to cross over into the destiny that you have called me.
2. Father, every destiny blocker, stopper, destroyer that have come to provoke me, may you provoke that spirit in the Mighty name of Jesus.
3. My Father, my Father, may you push me into that prepared place of victory in the name of Jesus Christ.
4. Oh Lord my God, let the rhythm of my worship fill your temple in the mighty name of Jesus.
5. Father in the mighty name of Jesus I break, cancel and dismantle every spirit that have come to destroy, stop me, narrow my path and to slow me down, I decree and declare that I am not ordinary, I am extra-ordinary through the blood of Jesus, and moulded by the hands that have the nail prints.
6. Father, I now decree and declare that my feet are like hinds feet, wherever I go, I shall have dominion and authority in the name of Jesus. Every dart that have been set up in my path to destroy me let that spiritual hinds feet begin to crush every symbol of the enemy in the name of Jesus.
7. Oh Lord my God I thank you now for my tongue is a ready writer I will write my destiny and I will watch it come to pass. Father, I am a generational curse breaker in the name of Jesus.

8. I _____________________(your name) am a forerunner for my generation and I shall fly through troupes and leap over wall because the leaper's grace is upon me to leap into success, victory, into the unknown with power and authority in the name of Jesus.

9. Oh Lord let my thunderous applause of victory reach the ears of mine enemies, let it be an atomic bomb against every evil altar that is set up against my generation in the name of Jesus.

10. Lord my Father I am ready to accelerate into my next level. I decree and declare that in this season I am anointed and appointed for my next level. Let the anointing power of Almighty God catapult me into victory because victory is mine.

Day 19: Declaration

1. Oh Lord, I have been through some valleys, hit rock bottom, gone through some deep weather, but I decree and declare that my double portion is now here, in Jesus Christ name.

2. Oh God my Father! My Father! You said, "I am come to deliver, set free, break the yokes and lift every heavy burden off me." I now stand in confidence that It does not matter how much I have cried in the past; my double is certain.

3. The mission impossible is possible in this atmosphere. Oh Lord, oh Lord by fire contend with my contender. Lord every evil one that has been listed against my life break by fire. Every sceptre of the enemy break by fire.

4. Every evil tree that the enemy has planted, every evil tree that my father did not plant be uprooted, uprooted. Every evil fruit tree be uprooted from my life, my generation, my marriage, ministry. Be uprooted now by fire in the name of Jesus Christ.

5. Scorpions from heaven move into the hiding places of my oppressors and expose their weaknesses, bite them mercilessly until they have no life in them , in Jesus name.

6. Scorpions from heaven, arise! Fight my battles. Let every scorpion from hell assigned to bite me, and derail my destiny, be overcome by your mighty sting and be destroyed now, in Jesus Christ Name.

7. Hear me when I call upon your name Oh God, may you hide me from the conspiracy of the secret council of the wicked and from the insurrection of the workers of iniquity, in Jesus Mighty name.

8. I now decree and declare that every secret evil shooter that operate in silence against me; as they bend their bow let it back-fire at them, in Jesus Mighty name.

9. Father, every evil contenders and sabotagers that have ridden over my head and caused for me to go through: fire, traps, and deep waters; may you cause them to die by fire but bring me out through the door of wealth as my permanent state in Jesus Mighty name.

10. Oh Mighty God of battles and war, see every rebellious altars that are erected against my destiny, and now my Father by the blast of your nostril, scatter their evil projections in Jesus Mighty name.

Day 20: Declaration

1. Oh Lord even nature responds to you, let the east wind, west wind, north wind begin to blow furiously and blow away every fake double trouble showing up in my life, in Jesus name.
2. I decree and declare that every contrary wind blowing strange sounds against my life, sounding like death, be silenced now in the name of Jesus Christ! I cannot be destroyed if God is for me who can be against me?
3. Oh you mighty warrior, your ship may be rocking from side to side, the sails are torn from the battering of the raging storms of life, the boisterous winds have threatened your peace, but you shall not die, you shall rest in the eye of the storm.
4. Let your blood bleed upon my life, for deliverance and freedom from every torture, captivity, oppression, and evil spirit in Jesus Mighty name.
5. Lord, turn every stronghold into victory of freedom for me, every prisoner: garment, position, mind-set I command a loosing, let there be double for my trouble according to Zechariah 9:12, in Jesus Mighty name.
6. I decree and declare that the warrior in me shall come alive and fight for victory in the name of Jesus Christ.
7. Every evil tree that the enemy planted against my life shall not bear fruit, it shall be uprooted now in Jesus Christ name.

8. Neighbour I decree and declare that your umbilical chord shall be connected only to the true vine of righteousness in the name of Jesus Christ.

9. We declare war, by fire by force we call upon the name of the God of Elijah to execute judgment against your haters who plot and fight against you, in Jesus name.

10. Oh Almighty God whose voice is like the sound of many waters, let the voice of your blood speak out over every area of my life and vanquish every other blood sacrifice lifted against me in Jesus Christ Mighty name.

Day 21: Declaration

1. Father in the name of Jesus Christ, I take back my prayer life now and trample upon every serpent, every Leviathan that are working to suck me dry; receive fire right now, right now, right now! My next level is here.

2. By prophetic decree I step into new dimensions in every area of my life and declare newness is my divine portion.

3. Oh Lord I decree and declare that I am too hot for any spirit of lethargicness and laziness to be attached to me, I command the fire of God to rage in every department of my life in Jesus name.

4. I decree and declare that I walk in the supernatural dimension of faith, I am unstoppable, I am incomprehensible because I am crazy enough to believe that my wait is over, although the storms are still raging.

5. Today I buckle up my seat belt, as I take off on the eagle's flight of new dimensions, my feet have graced new territories, a winning attitude and a nothing is impossible with God mindset is upon me, in Jesus name.

6. Oh God of Elijah let your fire begin to war on my behalf; burn, cancel dismantle every evil scepter that has risen up against me, in the name of Jesus Christ.

7. Oh God I come in agreement with your word, that I shall

decree a thing and watch it manifest, I command brimstone and fire to burn and shatter every evil altar that is erected against my life.

8. I decree and declare that it is my winning season, I do not entertain failure or defeat, I reject all negativity, I have already crossed over Jordan and I am into my Canaan of abundance and peace.

9. I command Godly appointed kingdom investors and destiny helpers to align themselves to me for the forwarding of the kingdom of God, in Jesus Mighty name.

10. I prophesy that out of my belly shall flow rivers of living water, mighty miracles, signs and wonders shall flow from me, because I no longer operate in the realm of the what if. But the it is already done!

Bonus 1: Declaration

1. Oh Lord, I make a declaration in the heavens that no sabotaging Laban spirit shall change my wages, I release the flying scroll against every thief of my inheritance in Jesus Christ name.

2. You spirit of the emptier, I address you under the power of the Holy Ghost, By fire I command you to return every stolen property with interest in Jesus mighty name.

3. I bind the spirit of victimization, and crush the serpent's head of every destiny waster, and command a divine seven fold restitution by executive order, in Jesus name.

4. I decree and declare that my detractors shall behold my overflowing blessings, and can neither say good or evil concerning me because God has shut their mouths.

5. Every conniving serpent pretending to be a friend, to suck my virtues, I command the fire of God to locate you now, and burn you to ashes in Jesus Christ Mighty name.

6. You evil conspirator, collecting information on my life to bring me down, I release the power of the blood of Jesus Christ against you evil enterprise, receive fire and destruction now in Jesus Christ Mighty name.

7. Oh manipulative deceiver, I come against you in the wrath and fire of God, receive his judgment and disgrace in Jesus

Mighty name.

8. I decree and declare that although you have been victimized your victory is right here. It is your time. Your time has come and now is the season that you shall be celebrated, because your father will be capitalized in Jesus Name.

9. I decree and declare that I arise out of every dunghill, victimization, sabotage, set-backs, delays and rise to sweet victory through the power of the cross in Jesus Christ name.

10. By exicutive order, I command every firce winds to cease, every diabolical cyclone to scatter by fire and a great tsumani to enter the store house of the theif and return every stolen blessings to me now, in the Mighty Name of Jesus!

Bonus 2: Declaration

1. Oh Glory Hallelujah! I was only victimized for God to be capitalized, victory is in my cup.
2. Father, in this hour of breakthroughs and deliverance, smite with your mighty fist every Amalekite, Midianite, Jebusite, Amorite, Girgashite spirits, scatter their work of darkness by fire, in Jesus name.
3. Oh Lord, may you remember me in my deep distress, let not the enemies laugh and pout their mouths saying, where is your God? Arise and defend me and break the rods of the enemies in Jesus Christ Mighty name.
4. I decree and declare that the Lord is with me as a mighty and terrible one: therefore, my persecutors shall stumble, and they shall not prevail: they shall be greatly ashamed; for they shall not prosper: their everlasting confusion shall never be forgotten.
5. I arise and open my mouth and declare a holy war against every oppression of the enemy. I am not your candidate for defeat, victory is in my DNA, I release an atomic bomb against every evil altar, seeking my demise, scatter and burn to irrepairable pieces in Jesus Christ Mighty name.
6. By the mighty Word of God I uproot my faith from a lodebar position to an Ararat height of promise. In the midst of

seeming failures, I declare that God has already turned every distress around, the waters have asswaged and that is my covenant of promise!

7. Oh covenant keeping God of irrevocable promises, let your rainbow be stretched visibly across every flood in my life as a reminder that affliction cannot arise a second time, only victory is allowed, in Jesus name.

8. I decree and declare that I shall prosper and have good success, because I will observe and obey the word of God.

9. I decree and declare that because I am fruitful, I multiply and take charge of every region and territory, that my feet shall trod. The enemies shall shake and be dumb-founded for they shall see that the Lord is with me, like a great and terrible one.

10. By executive order I command every fierce winds to cease, every diabolical cyclone to scatter by fire, and a great tsunami to enter the store house of the thief and return every stolen blessings to me, now in Jesus mighty name.

Bonus 3: Declaration

1. Oh Lord, I stand upon your promises today, your hands are not short where you cannot save, neither your ears heavy that you cannot hear, let a mighty double-double of everything I loss hit my life now in Jesus name.

2. I command every waters of disappointments, bad news, ill-spoken words, charismatic witchcraft, to reverse and dump in the sea of your wrath in Jesus name.

3. Oh covenant keeping God, may you arise in this hour and have respect unto your covenant with me, let every deep waters of set-backs and sabotage threatening my peace be abated now in Jesus Christ name.

4. Lord give me your word, establish your word in me. Jesus break down barriers and loose me into new dimension.

5. Lord break me free from every spirit of abandonment, bondage, every ancestral curse I am free by the blood of Jesus Christ. I declare grace upon me. New mindset is upon me.

6. Every dry tree that has my name on it receive fire now, ashes to ashes dust to dust. Let my fruit trees be fruitful with multiplication, in the name of Jesus.

7. Father, I now decree and declare that the bless shall call me bless, let there be a 24 hour watch upon my walls and instant multiple break-throughs shall locate me in Jesus name.

8. Where is the God of Elijah? God of fire every suppression that has been done against my life die by fire! By fire! By fire! Break! Break! Break! Hallelujah!

9. My Father, my Father arise in your anger and fight against every mouth piece speaking against my life and destiny in Jesus mighty name.

10. Oh Lord I declare that with your double portion, I am not ordinary, when I walk the enemies sniff the blood of Jesus on me and every demon have to scream out, get out and scatter by fire!

Morning Dew: A 30-Day
Devotional and Declaration
Refreshment

Made in the USA
Middletown, DE
27 January 2025

70021480R00117